It's 11:59 and the Bridegroom is Coming!

*Priority*ONE
p u b l i c a t i o n s

Detroit, Michigan USA

Contents

Preface

"It's 11:59 and the Bridegroom is Coming" was birthed after the Holy Spirit put it on my heart to write a book about the forthcoming of the Bridegroom (Jesus) to catch away the saints. As you see, I obeyed.

I make no claims about knowing when Jesus will come. No one knows the date or the hour of His appearance. I take no stand regarding a pre-millennial, mid-millennial, or post-millennial rapture of the church. My instruction from the Holy Spirit in 2010 was to write a book entitled "It's 11:59 and the Bridegroom Is Coming." I am to remind the people that It's 11:59 and the Bridegroom will come at midnight. The Holy Spirit said, "The purpose of the Bible is to show My people how history repeats itself. I want My people to learn from past failures and to not repeat the evil injustices that have been committed by man. If they won't learn from them they will be judged."

Bible prophecy has interested me since I was a child. My family's church denomination believed and preached about future prognostications, so it seems I have always believed that God had a plan for each of us. And since He had a plan for our lives that meant that He had foreknowledge about what would happen in the future, I reasoned.

Another thing that fascinated me was the fact that ministers rarely talked about the major events that have already occurred in the world as the fulfillment of prophecy. In school I learned about the world wars, the monarchies of the past, Christopher Columbus' discovery of America, etc.; but I could not connect it to what I was learning in church.

The discussion of Bible prophecy is no longer limited to the inside walls of one or two denominations. You can turn on television or any other media and hear people prophesying the future of the world. There are many notable ministers, prophets, teachers and televangelists connecting current events to Bible prophecy.

In writing "It's 11:59 and the Bridegroom Is Coming," I provide many related scriptures from the King James, Amplified, and New Living Bible translations for clarity. In addition, there is a plethora of historical information that I believe is related to the fulfillment of Bible prophecy.

As a servant of the Most High God, I have followed the instruction of the Holy Spirit to the best of my ability. I make no claims to be a Bible scholar. I just love the Lord with all my heart and I'm available for Him to use me as He desires. I therefore dedicate "It's 11:59 and the Bridegroom is Coming" to the Most High God.

Introduction

Many people find it hard to believe that the way things are will drastically change in the near future. The signs are everywhere that we are in the last days of this age and the Bridegroom is almost ready to pick up His Bride, the Body of Christ.

The Ten Commandments, the regulations written by God in Exodus 20 and given to the children of Israel, were once recognized worldwide as the core value system for humanities' behavior. Their acceptance has deteriorated and is declining rapidly to record lows. It is a time when evil, deviant behavior is supported and promoted while virtuous and righteous behaviors are depreciated and criticized. Laws written to support virtuous behaviors are being overturned and replaced with laws supporting behaviors formally viewed as deviant. Jesus is coming to earth again, what if it were today?

The Bible speaks of a time when the nations will stand in judgment before God. Jesus said: *All nations will be gathered before Him, and He will separate them [the people] from one another as a shepherd separates his sheep from the goats; And He will cause the sheep to stand at His right hand, but the goats at the left. Then the King will say to those at His right hand, Come, you blessed of My Father [you favored of God and appointed to eternal salvation], inherit (receive as your own) the kingdom prepared for you from the foundation of the world* (Matthew 25:32-34 AMP).

Part of what I've been called to do in this book is to compare Bible prophecy to history and identify when prophecy has been fulfilled. Events have occurred in the world that may have escaped the attention of those who study eschatology. Through "It's 11:59 and the Bridegroom Is Coming," I am sounding an alarm to change your mind and purpose to accept God's way instead of rebelling against His way of doing things before it is too late.

The signs are everywhere that the catching away of Christians is imminent.

It will happen in a moment, in the blinking of an eye, when the last trumpet is blown.

For when the trumpet sounds, the Christians who have died will be raised with transformed bodies. And then we who are living will be transformed so that we will never die (I Corinthians 15:52 (NLT).

1

That Which Was and is to Come

The time is 11:59 and the trumpet is set to sound at midnight. Christians are taught to hope and be comforted in the knowledge that Jesus will return and take them to Heaven where He resides. Although no one on earth knows the day or hour of Jesus' appearing we know from the fulfillment of Bible prophecy when compared to historical events, the catching away (Rapture) of the saints and the return of the Lord is imminent.

Just imagine, I Thessalonians 4:16-18 describes a time soon when Jesus will leave Heaven and appear in the air with His angels. The angels will blow their trumpets and will sing while announcing the appearance of our Savior and Lord. Jesus will shout something like "Come up here." In obedience to His command the saints of God who are already dead will arise from their graves and meet the Lord in the air. It does not matter if they were cremated and their ashes are sitting on the mantle in an urn or if their remains disappeared in war. Their bodies will come together supernaturally at the Savior's command, and then those saints who are alive will ascend to meet the Savior in the air. Afterward, the saints of God will stay with the Lord.

The title "It's 11:59" implies with urgency that mankind is on a biblical timetable when this great event will occur. If the fullness of time for the Rapture was set in Heaven for midnight then Jesus' return is about to happen. To ward off confusion, "It's 11:59 and the Bridegroom is Coming" does not relate to the Second Coming of Christ when He will touch down on the Mount of Olives and set up His kingdom on earth. This event was forecasted while Jesus was ascending into Heaven. Two men (possibly angels) told the disciples:

> ...Men of Galilee, why do you stand gazing into heaven? This same Jesus, Who was caught away and lifted up from among you

into heaven, will return in [just] the same way in which you saw Him go into heaven (Acts 1:11 AMP).

This refers to the Second Coming of Christ.

In this book, references to the end of the age or "the latter days," refer to the time and events before the catching away of the Body of Christ and the Tribulation period. Previously fulfilled prophecies indicate the Rapture of the Church is at hand. Please note with urgency, billions of people are still not saved. The "last days" actually began on the Day of Pentecost more than 2,000 years ago according to the Apostle Peter in Acts 2:17. Folks, we are in the last days.

Nations in Transition

While the earth remains, the world system will transition into "a New World Order." Nations will change their boundaries and possibly names. Even now there are talks of Iran changing its name back to Persia. Currently there is civil war in Syria, and there is discontent in Libya, Egypt and other Middle Eastern countries. Furthermore there are riots and discontent over the economy in America, France, Greece and other European Union nations.

As we study the history of nations we see how they have changed. For example, the British Empire was called such because it ruled many colonies all over the world. However, many of its colonies have now become independent nations.

[1]Look at the Roman Empire, it governed for more than 400 years. Based in Italy, it ruled over the modern day nations of the United Kingdom, Andorra, France, Belgium, Netherlands, Spain, Portugal, Switzerland, Austria, Hungary, parts of Germany, Romania, Bulgaria, Greece, Turkey, Israel, Syria, Arabia, Tunisia, Algeria, Monaco, Luxembourg, Liechtenstein, San Marino, the Vatican City, Malta, Slovenia, Croatia, Bosnia-Herzegovina, Yugoslavia, Albania, FYR Macedonia, Armenia, Iraq, Cyprus, Lebanon, Jordan, Egypt, Palestine (as part of the Roman Province of Judaea), and Morocco.

The Roman Empire will be revived in the "last days" according to prophecy in Daniel 2 and 7. [2]The revived Roman Empire could be the European Union (EU). The EU's current nations include Austria, Belgium, Bulgaria, Republic of Cyprus, Czech Republic, Denmark, Estonia, Finland, France, Greece, Hungary, Ireland, Italy, Latvia, Lithuania,

Luxembourg, Malta, Netherlands, Poland, Portugal, Romania, Slovakia, Slovenia, Spain, Sweden, the United Kingdom and Germany. Notably, the following nations are not a part of the EU as yet: Iraq, Lebanon, Jordan, Egypt, Syria, Algeria, Arabia, Tunisia, and Turkey. I'll let you decide if the current members of the EU resemble the former Roman Empire named above. Scripture says the earth will remain providing seed time and harvest. The nations will continue to thrive until Jesus establishes His kingdom on earth.

After being in office for 30 years, Egypt's president Hosni Mubarak handed his power to the military government in February 2011. After 18 days the people chanted: "The people ousted the president through non-violent protest." After a highly contested election on June 30, 2012, Mohammed Morsi was voted in and officially declared president of the Arab Republic of Egypt. President Morsi was in office until he was declared unseated on July 3, 2013, by opposition forces. Politics in Egypt is in crisis with no clear leadership. It seems that the military is now in charge. (From unconfirmed Internet sources.)

Rebel forces ousted Syria's long-term president, Muammar Gadhafi in August 2011. Gadhafi was killed on Oct. 20, 2011, after being captured by the National Transition Council. There is still rioting and what looks like a civil war in the streets of Syria because people are dissatisfied with the current leader, President Bashar Assad. News.Yahoo/un-more reported that more than 100,000 people are dead because of Syria's civil war. The country is in a state of chaos.

The United States for the most part has supported the nation of Israel in its decision-making policies. However in 2011, President Barack Obama and Israeli Prime Minister Benjamin Netanyahu disagreed whether Israel must move its borders back to where it was prior to the 1967 war for a new Palestinian state. So you see the nations will always be at odds about something and these disagreements sometimes lead to war.

The winds of change have been released throughout the world. Governments, industries, institutions, ideologies, educational institutions and every entity involving mankind are being rearranged, and I speculate, for the entry of the "man of sin"—the Antichrist. More than likely, he is currently alive and being groomed for his position on the world stage.

Solomon, the wisest man outside of Jesus, said: *The thing that hath been, it is that which shall be; and that which is done is that which shall be done: and there is no new thing under the sun* (Ecclesiastes 1:9). From the beginning of the world nations have disagreed and fought each other; nothing has changed. However, wars and global troubles will intensify the closer we come to the end.

Deception in the World

Jesus warned the disciples: *...Be careful that no one misleads you [deceiving you and leading you into error]* (Matthew 24:4 AMP). We know satan's profession is to deceive; he is a deceiver and his job is to steal, kill, and destroy (John 10:10). Deception is a chief weapon in his arsenal. He was a deceiver from the beginning. He deceived a third of the angels to rebel against God and follow him. He also deceived Eve to eat fruit from the tree thus condemning mankind to a lifetime of misery and death.

Satan is shrewd and will use our own spiritual weapons of warfare against us. Take heed to all of the different translations of the Bible that are currently being marketed. Some have changed the words of key doctrines of the Christian faith. For example, one translation calls Mary, the mother of Jesus, a maid. It makes no mention of the fact that she was a virgin (someone who never had sexual intercourse). A maid may not be a virgin. It is very important to understand that Mary had never been with a man; she was a holy vessel unto the Lord. The King James Bible tells the prophecy of a virgin's conception: *Therefore the Lord himself shall give you a sign; Behold, a Virgin shall conceive, and bear a son, and shall call his name Immanuel* (Isaiah 7:14). The prophecy was fulfilled in Matthew 1:18: *Now the birth of Jesus Christ was on this wise: When as his mother Mary was espoused to Joseph, before they came together, she was found with child of the Holy Ghost* .

The translations that call Mary a maid may lead to a misunderstanding of Jesus' birth credentials that are absolutely important to Christian doctrine. There are those who refuse to believe that a virgin could conceive a child without the help of a man. But they underestimate the powers of our Creator God. They do not understand that He is supernatural; a God without limitations. There is nothing too hard for Him

The enemy of our soul, satan, has deceived many by causing them to renounce their belief in compliance with the world's system. How did believers slide down the slippery slope of disobedience in exchange for secular worldly influences? There is no one answer but we will explore several factors that may have led to their indifference to obeying God's will as written in the Bible.

Abandonment of one's faith may occur so subtly that it is hardly noticeable. People who once were believers will be deceived by influences other than the Spirit of God. After they leave their faith, some will call them backsliders and or apostates. Let us explore our world and identify some reasons believers may leave their Christian faith.

Paul warns against the falling away from the faith of some believers because of counterfeit doctrines. One misrepresentation that is prevalent today is the belief that there is more than one way to get to Heaven. But Jesus said: *I am the Way the Truth and the Life; no one comes to the Father except by (through) Me* (John 14:6 AMP). This verse corrects any misunderstanding about their being multiple pathways to reach the Father God Almighty. Jesus is the only way to the Father.

Likewise, Luke said: *There is salvation in and through no one else, for there is no other name under heaven given among men by and in which we must be saved* (Acts 4:12 AMP).

Another false teaching that is very popular is that there is no hell, so when you die that is the end of you; plus a loving God would never send any person to hell. The Lord is not sending anyone to everlasting damnation. However, He has given the world His owner's manual, the Bible, considered by some to mean: Basic Instructions Before Leaving Earth. It contains everything you need to live a life of holiness for which He requires. When God's creation adheres to His leadership, their reward is eternal life with Him in Heaven. Those who choose to reject or deny Him and His Word willingly accept their reward of separation from God.

Hell was not created for mankind; it was created for satan and his angels and those who decide to follow him. If you reject the true and living God you get satan's judgment. (Scriptures about eternal life are found in the Appendix.)

An additional deception that exists is that it is acceptable to engage in sexual activity outside of the marriage covenant. Still there are others who believe that practicing perverted sex of every description is tolerable and acceptable. Notably, one's natural inclination is to satisfy the carnal or sensual nature with every indulgence imaginable. It does not matter if our sovereign God calls it a sin or transgression against His Word. The carnal nature is where evil thrives, which is contrary to the loving, forgiving nature of God. The Bible says the wages of sin is death (Romans 6:23). The manifestation of such carnal behavior that lead to eternal and sometimes physical death include unforgiveness, sexual immorality, impure thoughts, eagerness for lustful pleasure, idolatry, participation in demonic activities, hostility, quarreling, jealousy, outbursts of anger, selfish ambition, divisions, the feeling that everyone is wrong except those in your own little group, envy, drunkenness, wild parties and other kinds of sin. (See Galatians 5:19-21.)

Then there are those who believe that after one dies they go into a holding place of temporary punishment in which the souls of those who died in grace must atone for their sins. I cannot find any place in the Christian Bible to support such belief. However, Hebrews 9:27 says: *It is appointed unto men once to die, but after this the judgment.* The Word of God speaks for itself.

Another deception emphasizes human value above godly values. Seducing spirits of human rights is leading to a belief system that endorses everybody doing what is right in their own eyes. Many people in today's society live together instead of getting married. Laws are even being revised to legalize such immoral practices; the moral factor has already been overruled. It's sad to say there are so-called Christian denominations that are endorsing these ungodly behaviors. Their consciences are cauterized just as it was prophesied in I Timothy 4:1-3. These people have committed apostasy, falling away from the true doctrines of the faith.

Unfortunately, there are people attending church every week living in denial of true holiness. They may be attending church with ulterior motives such as to make business connections, to prey on unsuspecting young women (or men)—for reasons other than worshipping and serving the Lord. They are deceived.

False Religions

Countless people are deceived from the faith by the misrepresentations of false religious cults and secret societies. Religions that do not embrace the deity of Christ or believe in the necessity of His blood as the only way of atonement for sin are deceived and being used as a tool of satan. Following is a list of such religious organizations that include but are not limited to: Baha'i by Bahaullah; Buddhism founder Prince Siddhartha Gautama (called the Buddha); Christian Science by Mary Baker Eddy; Church of Scientology by Saint Hill Manor; Confucianism by Confucius; Freemasonry (secret society); Hinduism; Islam founder Mohammed—one of the fastest growing religions in the world; Krishna by Hare Krishna; Mormonism by Joseph Smith; New Age; Secular Humanism; Shintoism; Taoism; and Transcendental Meditation by Maharishi Mahesh Yogi. The Lord said through Jeremiah:

> ... The *[false] prophets prophesy lies in My name. I sent them not, neither have I commanded them, nor have I spoken to them. They prophesy to you a false or pretended vision, a worthless divination [conjuring or practicing magic, trying to call forth the responses supposed to be given by idols], and the deceit of their own minds* (Jeremiah 14:14 AMP).

Beware of those who preach or teach an antichrist doctrine.

When we study the lives of the disciples we discover they were much like us. They were curious about their future, insecure; some were prideful, and ambitious. The disciples questioned Jesus about the signs of His return and the end of the world. They asked Him three questions: (1) When shall these things be? (2) What shall be the sign of Thy coming? (3) What shall be the sign of the end of the world? (Matthew 24:3).

There Will Be False Sightings of Christ

Jesus told His disciples in Matthew 24:5 that false Messiahs would appear in His name and many would be misled. He warned them against this deception. The list of those who claim to be the Messiah and/or Jesus is inexhaustible. Some of the people who've claimed to be the Messiah include: [3]Sun Myung Moon (b. 1920), founder of the Unification Church, said he was the Second Coming of Christ; Father Divine (George Baker) (c. 1880-Sept. 10, 1965), an African American spiritual leader who claimed to be God from 1907 until his death in 1965; Jung Myung Seok (b.1945), founder of Providence Church and a convicted rapist, also claims to be the Second Coming of Christ. David Shayler, (b. 1965), former M15 agent and whistleblower, declared himself the Messiah on July 7, 2007. Laszlo Toth claimed he was Christ as he battered Michelangelo's *Pieta* with a geologist hammer. Akhenaten, Buddha, John Lenin and Father Divine also claimed to be the Messiah. Jim Jones (b. 1913-Nov. 18, 1978) claimed to be the reincarnation of Jesus and organized a mass-murder/suicide at Jonestown, Guyana. However, it was never proven that he died in the massacre.

False teachers not only deceive people but they usually incorporate some form of immorality, greed and lying into their deceptive practices. Many cults may involve and condone pedophilia, adultery, unlawful marriage to multiple women, and even children. They are antichrist in their beliefs and claim to have the Lord's power and authority, but don't.

Please note that whenever you look for signs you become susceptible to being deceived because satan has the ability to manipulate truth. Studying the Christian Bible under the guidance of a respected Holy Spirit-filled teacher will keep you from being deceived. You must also study the Bible independently!

Wars and Rumors of Wars (Matthew 25:6)

It is important to trace world history and understand there have always been wars even from the beginning of time. However wars have intensified and will continue to do so until Jesus and His heavenly hosts fight the final war, Armageddon. It will be a war between the forces of good and evil. Jesus said *Nation shall rise against nation, and kingdom against kingdom* (Luke 21:10). As I write this book, the nations are realigning against each other as we hear of possible wars between Israel and Iran. There is civil war in Syria, and the United States is at odds with Russia and China on how to resolve it.

To illustrate that these wars are the fulfillment of prophecy and will continue with greater intensity, I will recap some of the wars and fatalities that have already taken place. The United States participated in the following 19th, 20th, and 21st-century wars: U.S. Civil War (approximately 500,000 people were killed. World War I involved Austria, Hungary, Russia, Germany, France, Belgium, Britain, Bulgaria, Rumania, and Italy. Nation against nation: Germany, France, England, Italy, Russia, Japan, Poland, Manchuria and Ethiopia. Thirty nations were involved and it lasted four years, from 1914-1918; more than 20 million died both military and civilians. Notably, poison gas was used for the first time. WWI cost untold billions of dollars, ravaged Europe, knocked down kings and emperors and sowed the seeds for World War II.

[5] The next war was World War II. It was the most destructive war ever fought in the world to date. It lasted for six years, from 1939-1945. The countries

that fought in this war include the former Soviet Union, France, China, Great Britain, the United States, Italy, and Japan. More than 16 million military personnel were killed, although some believe at least 52 million people lost their lives in this war.

Nuclear Weapons

The invention of the atomic bomb in the 20th Century changed the methodology of how war is conducted. The use of the atom bomb in WWII was the first war in which a noncombatant population was targeted.

[6] When the U.S. bombed Hiroshima on Aug. 6, 1945, within two to four months approximately 90,000-166,000 people lost their lives and when they bombed the city of Nagasaki on Aug. 9, 1945, between 60,000-80,000 people died in that city. Thousands more died later from radiation related burns and diseases.

Americans lived under the threat of nuclear war during a period called the "Cold War." It was the era after WWII in 1945 through 1991 when the former Soviet Union and United States engaged in hostile relations, which threatened the world with a nuclear war. The Cold War was primarily between the United States and the Union of Soviet Socialist Republics (USSR) and ceased when the Soviet Union collapsed in 1991.

A memorable time for me was in 1962 during the Cuban missile crisis. Cuba adopted the Communist ideology and the Soviets attempted to aid their defenses by sending them nuclear missiles. Simply put, after much military and diplomatic pressure the Soviets agreed to remove the missiles if the U.S. agreed to not invade Cuba again. The potential nuclear war was averted. As a teenager I was terrified because I thought it would be the end of the world.

The closer we get to the end of the age the more we will hear about wars and rumors of wars. But Revelation 9:15 speaks of the war of wars in which a third of mankind will be killed; that war has yet to be fought. Wars will intensify the closer we are to the end.

Earthquakes in Various Places
(Matthew 24:7)

Numerous quakes have occurred throughout the world since the year 365 AD. The seismograph instrument was created in 1958 to measure and record vibrations within the earth. One quake that may be familiar to you happened in December 2004 in Southeast Asia. The quake triggered a tsunami that killed more than 250,000 people and left millions homeless in surrounding nations.

There is speculation that more than 220,000 people lost their lives in the Haitian earthquake of 2010. There was an earthquake in Chile just south of the capital of Santiago on Feb. 27, 2010, which registered 8.8 on the Richter scale. The U.S. Geological Survey reported an earthquake that measured a 6.9 magnitude in Southern Qinghai, China, killing 2,698 people and injuring thousands of others on April 13, 2010. Many people were also reported missing.

There were frequent earthquakes in 2011 across the globe. One quake which registered 8.9 on the Richter scale, occurred on March 11, 2011, and triggered a tsunami in Japan. More than 18,000 people were killed. There were also significant earthquakes in 2011 in America (Alaska and Virginia), Indonesia and Turkey. However the greatest earthquakes are yet to come according to Revelation 6:12, 11:13, and 16:18.

Storms and Natural Disasters

[8]On Nov. 12, 2012, the Washington Post blogs reported "Venice flooding swamps 70% of city" by Jason Samenow. He reported Venice, Italy, reached its sixth-highest level since 1872.

In October 2012, Hurricane Sandy (called the Superstorm) smashed against the Atlantic East Coast region causing horrendous damage extending from the Caribbean Islands throughout the northeastern part of the United States. Hurricane Sandy is estimated to be the second most costly hurricane in U.S. history, surpassed only by Hurricane Katrina in 2005. The death toll was more than 100. This was a very unusual weather event that devastated New Jersey and New York. It is estimated that 8 million people were without power.

During 2011, America was ravaged with an unprecedented number of tornadoes with more than

550 fatalities. In addition, the Mississippi River flooded in multiple states destroying everything in its path, including homes and farmland. According to Gene Rench of the National Weather Service, it was the worst flooding of the Mississippi River in 500 years. In late October 2011, there were major snowstorms that dropped up to two feet of snow in the Northeast. More than 3 million homes and businesses were without electricity for days. Floods killed nearly 1,000 people in Brazil.

The people impacted by these storms had to depend on the government to rescue them financially until their insurance companies were able to assess the damage and compensate them. Record numbers of people affected were poor and didn't have insurance because of the recession. The burden on the government was billions of dollars for 12 weather disasters. "Natural disasters, such as tornadoes, hurricanes and earthquakes represent a far greater threat to the economy than terrorism," according to insurance financier Warren Buffet who was quoted in an article written by Ash Lingers in Reuters ("Economy Impact to Rise Sharply," April 19, 2010). Hurricane

Katrina did an estimated $125 billion-$200 billion in damage.

Japan's earthquake and tsunami caused an estimated $300 billion in damage. As of Sept. 11, 2011, a total of 15,839 people had died, according to the National Police Agency of Japan (from wiki.answers.com 1/13/2012).

Thailand suffered the worst flooding in half a century. Approximately 373 people were killed and 2.5 million lives were disrupted. (Reuters 10/28/2011.)

[9]In 2010, the Iceland volcano (Eyjafiallajökull) shut down a great portion of the world's airplane travel routes. The eruptions began April 14, 2010, and because the volcanic ash that erupted from the volcano had spewed across Europe, more than 100,000 flights were cancelled. The airlines expected to lose more than $2 billion. When the Iceland volcano erupted, people on the continents of Africa, Europe and North America discovered they were mere humans and the situation was outside of their control; planes were grounded for more than a week. There was so much smoke and ash spewing from the volcano that it reached about 55,000 feet in the air. Flights were

grounded for fear that the explosive ash would clog the engines of the planes and cause them to shut down.

[10] In 1970 a cyclone and accompanying storm surge killed an estimated 500,000 people in Bangladesh. In 1923 in Japan about 130,000 people were killed in an earthquake in Tokyo and Yokohama. A 7.9 quake in China in 2008 caused 69,000 to 87,000 deaths.

It was almost as if God was letting people know that they were not in charge. The closer we get to the end of the age the more earthquake activities will intensify. The greatest earthquake will take place at the very end of the age.

There will be Famines and Pestilences
(Matthew 24:7)

It is important to examine history to see if Bible prophecies have manifested. There have been major plagues across the earth from 1347 through 1700. The Black Death Bubonic Plague struck Europe and the Mediterranean area, killing millions. This plague was also called a "pestilence."

[11] Let's look at the pandemic pestilence: The "Spanish" Influenza virus pandemic swept the globe and killed between 20 and 40 million people between 1918 and 1919.

Tuberculosis, also a pestilence, kills millions of people annually. The HIV/AIDS epidemic for which there is no known cure is also looked upon as a pestilence and is considered to be the deadliest epidemic in human history. According to the World Health Organization, from 1981 to November 2005, more than 25 million people have died as a result of AIDS. In 2007, there were 33 million people living with the disease; 2.1 million adults and children died of AIDS that same year.

Even though we don't have exact figures, untold millions have died in Africa from pestilence famines. Unfortunately, millions are still dying as we speak.

Christian Persecution

Jesus told the disciples they would suffer persecution (Matthew 24:9). After being blessed by Him, the disciples obeyed His commands, remained in Jerusalem and received the blessing of the Holy Spirit as cited in Acts 2:1-4. They took the Gospel to the world and later were martyred for their Christian witness.

Stephen was a man chosen by the apostles to be a servant in the church. *And Stephen, full of faith and power, did great wonders and miracles among the people* (Acts 6:8).

Stephen was martyred, being stoned to death after defending the faith in Jesus Christ (Acts 7:58-60). According to *"Foxe's Christian Martyrs of the World,"* by John Foxe, all the apostles but John were martyred:

- ➤ Stephen was stoned to death.
- ➤ Simon, the apostle, was crucified.
- ➤ John Mark was burned and buried before he was killed.
- ➤ James was beheaded.
- ➤ Bartholomew was beheaded.
- ➤ Matthew was speared to death.
- ➤ Philip was crucified.
- ➤ James, the brother of Jesus, was bludgeoned to death.
- ➤ Peter was crucified upside down.

"Death was not considered enough
punishment for the Christians, who were
subjected to the cruelest treatment
possible. They were whipped,
disemboweled, torn apart, and strangled,
eaten by wild animals, hung, and tossed
on the horns of bulls. After they were
dead, their bodies were piled in heaps and
left to rot without burial. Nevertheless, the
Church continued to grow, deeply rooted
in the doctrine of the apostles and watered
with the blood of the saints." (Foxe's
Christian Martyrs of the World by John
Foxe, p.10.)

The number of Christians who were martyred
during the time of the early church is unknown; but
some say multitudes were killed because they believed
in Jesus as the Savior.

Five missionaries were killed in 1956 in the
Ecuadorian jungle. They were Nate Saint, Jim Elliot,
Ed McCully, Pete Fleming and Roger Youderian. They
committed themselves to obeying the will of God—to
spread the Gospel message throughout the world. The
five missionaries made plans to visit the Huaroriani
village (one of the more violent tribes) but were killed
by 10 Huaroriani men on January 8, 1956. They

became martyrs instantly. *Life Magazine* published a 10-page article on their mission and death. Jim Elliot wrote before his death: "He is no fool who gives what he cannot keep to gain what he cannot lose."

Missionaries have been revered for most of America's history. Unfortunately that is not the case in our contemporary culture. Missionaries are generally viewed as people who dropped out of the competitive secular world because they could not measure up. Sadly, very few young people set their career goals on becoming a missionary. Usually their goals are set to make lots of money so they can purchase plenty of stuff; thus fulfilling their dreams and those of their parents. A more heavenly goal would be sowing seeds of obedience to God's Word, which is His will and reaping His blessings, which last an eternity.

Christians are being persecuted right now all over the world. Because you don't hear about it does not mean it is not happening. Our brothers and sisters are suffering slavery and the horrors of persecution in Asia, Africa, India, China, the Island nations, and in Muslim countries.

I visited China twice as a missionary in the 1990s. We smuggled Bibles and various other

Christian materials into the country to enlighten and encourage the Chinese believers. These materials went to the vibrant underground churches. On one occasion we met with a pastor of an unregistered church, which is illegal in China according to Chinese law. He told us the story of how he was persecuted by being imprisoned off and on over a period of 12 years. He told us that he was beaten, tortured and sent to a rock quarry prison near Tibet. Throughout his imprisonment and persecution, he continued to spread the Gospel message to other inmates. Finally after prison authorities realized nothing short of death would stop him from telling people about Jesus, they released him. I felt so unworthy to even be in his presence. What a pleasure it was to meet such a humble man of God.

On another occasion we were secretly passing out Christian tracks in the Chinese language to people who passed us as we walked along a beautiful lily filled lagoon. As I passed a young lady, I slipped a track into her hand. The next thing I knew I was grabbed from behind and turned 180 degrees as she gave me a big hug, clutching her track close to her heart. As she held the track she was bowing, thanking me for her spiritual bread. She obviously knew the value of the track. We were told that the track would be copied multiple times and spread throughout the country. No Christian material is wasted or hoarded; it is shared so others may be converted. Believers are being targeted and losing their lives because they worship Jesus.

The Persian Gulf War was followed by the genocide of select ethnic groups. Many Christians, were gassed, shot or forced to leave their homes (Jesus Freaks p. 333.)

"Northern Nigeria's predominately Muslim population at times terrorizes Christians, destroying churches and killing believers, but the government previously has turned a blind eye to this injustice." (Jesus Freaks p. 342.) More than 27 Christians were killed and their churches bombed by a radical Muslim terrorist in central Nigeria on Christmas Day in 2011.

[12] There are reports in Pakistan that Christians are being slaughtered by Muslim mobs for being Christians and refusing to convert to Islam. (See article on pajamasmedia.com/phyllischesler/2009/08/12, "Open-season on Christians.") According to the article eight Christians were burned alive by a mob of

Muslims. Christians are also being persecuted in Sudan, Somalia, Nigeria, Turkey, Pakistan, Gaza and Iran.

It is important to identify what has occurred in the past and what is happening currently so you won't be caught off guard. The world powers seek to hide the real news by camouflaging it with silly, meaningless programming. Open your eyes and look at the real issues and events that do not receive much media attention. The enemy of your soul is a deceiver and seeks to steal, kill and destroy you by keeping you busy chatting about things that have no eternal value. You will encounter more distractions the closer we get to the end and the appearance of the Antichrist.

Beheadings

"Three Islamic militants (in Jakarta, India) were found guilty Wednesday of decapitating three Christian schoolgirls and dumping their bloodied heads in nearby villages, judges said. They were sentenced to between 14 and 20 years, according to an article published by the Associated Press on March 21, 2007 (http://www.foxnews.com).

John, the author of Revelation, wrote the following about those who were beheaded for Christ's sake: ...*And I saw the souls of them that were beheaded for the witness of Jesus, and for the word of God, and which had not worshipped the beast, neither his image, neither had received his mark upon their foreheads, or in their hands; and they lived and reigned with Christ a thousand years* (Revelations 20:4).

It saddens me to hear about religious persecution and harassment in this "so called Christian" nation. There seems to be a concerted effort to destabilize the practice of Christianity in America. Almost weekly we hear mentioned in the media something about our courts, governmental agencies and the ACLU (American Civil Liberties Union) challenging Christian practices in some respect. Your First Amendment right to practice the religion of your choice is guaranteed.

In a 2009 article in *Charisma* magazine, a California couple was fined $300 for holding a Bible Study in their home. There are numerous reports of incidents where people are prohibited from praying in public schools or at graduations. And if they are permitted to pray they cannot use the phrase, "in

Jesus name." On Feb. 3, 2010, two African American Christian men were shot and killed while witnessing on the streets in Boynton Beach, Fla. It is our First Amendment right to practice Christianity in America. Let us never forget it or stop exercising that right regardless of the devil's strategies to hinder us. Jesus told Peter in Matthew 16:18 that the gates of hell will not conquer His church.

You Better Be Ready

Jesus is coming for His Bride, the Body of Christ, the glorious Church. Therefore, it behooves Christians to stop participating in the fleshly activities of this world that distracts them from being all God created them to be. These distractions are strategic, deliberately planned by the enemy and include but are not limited to such things as excessive television, an obsession with social media, sexual immorality (including pornography), secret sins or addictions, greed, lust, selfishness, covetousness, jealousy, rebellion, unforgiveness, worldly ambitions, defiling the body with alcohol and or drugs (even prescription drugs), idolatry, hatred, unbelief and disobedience.

Dump your excess baggage at the foot of Jesus before it gets too heavy for lift off. Take yourself off the throne where God belongs. When Jesus says, "Come up hear," you don't want to be like Lot's wife and be left behind. You want to move when it is time to move. The author of Hebrews admonishes: ...*let us strip off and throw aside every encumbrance (unnecessary weight) and that sin which so readily (deftly and cleverly) clings to and entangles us, and let us run with patient endurance and steady and active persistence the appointed course of the race that is set before us* (Hebrews 12:1 AMP).

When I was a child I heard the old folks say Jesus was coming back to earth to pick up His believers. I would look at the cloud formation occasionally and could almost see Jesus sitting on His throne and the angels surrounding Him, blowing the trumpets. I am reminded that one day He will crack the sky and every eye will see Him.

There is a song that says, and I paraphrase, "Jesus is coming to Earth Again. What if it was today?" Are you ready for Jesus to come today?

It's 11:59 and the Bridegroom is coming!

2

Sin Will be Rampant Everywhere

Most people—Christians and non-Christians alike—are oblivious to the lateness of the hour as it relates to the "catching away" or Rapture of the Church. They go about their daily tasks without any thought of God or what He wants for their lives. The result is that they live their lives bent toward self-centeredness. In a secular worldview structure there is no place for a commitment to the true and living God. Therefore everyone does what is right in his or her own eyes. The following reveals the consequences of such thinking as it relates to the fulfillment of Bible prophecy.

Jesus warns: *And because iniquity (extreme immorality) shall abound the love of many shall wax (grow) cold* (Matthew 24:12, parenthesis mine). The word *cold* implies "insensitive," "unsympathetic," or "unemotional." The following article was written in the 1940s. Compare the concerns the United Lutheran Church had about sin then to today's church at large.

[1]"The committee on moral and social welfare of the United Lutheran Church, meeting in Philadelphia, some time ago, submitted a list of sixteen modern sins and urged the church to address its attention to these sins:

   1) Racketeering;

   2) Gambling;

   3) Exploitations;

   4) Bribery;

   5) Profanity;

   6) Dissipation;

   7) Diseases;

   8) Suicide;

   9) Sex-laxity;

   10) Lawlessness;

   11) Organized agencies within society have
      in large sections been perverted;

12) Infidelity between husbands and
wives, disloyalty between parents and
children, undisciplined temperaments;

13) Radical prejudices;

14) Jealousies, greed, grudges between
nationalities;

15) The wrong attitude of class toward
class in society;

16) Great wealth and luxury and abject
poverty within sight of each other but
separated by an impassable gulf;
leisure because of no need to work and
enforced idleness because of no
opportunity to work; the palace
towering over the hovel; privilege and
under privilege."

Unfortunately the sins have not changed but
have grown in intensity and in frequency; and because
our society has changed so drastically, some are not
even categorized as sin anymore.

The spirit of murder dominates the news today.
CNN recently reported a United Nations report during
2010 that estimated "global homicides at 468,000."
Murder rates, the report added, were highest in parts

of America and Africa, eight in 10 homicide victims were men, and most women were murdered at home.

U.S. crime statistics reflect a major increase in lawlessness from 1960 through 2010:

- Violent crime increased 432%
- Murder increased 162%
- Forcible rape increased 493%
- Burglary increased 237%
- Aggravated assault increased 505%

According to the "Time Almanac" (2010 pp. 618-619), there were 12,791 murders in America in 2009. In 2007, there were 2,013,180 prisoners and an estimated 14.2 million arrests. Just think of all the crime that was not reported. Crime seems to be getting more heinous and monstrous as we hear about the killing of entire families. The increase in crime is another pointer to the fulfillment of New Testament prophecies that Jesus is coming.

You can link the crime rate in America to the constant bombardment of lawlessness and immorality portrayed by the media 24 hours a day. The government and filmmakers were very protective about what they allowed us to hear or see in movies or on television when I was a child. The religious community was proactive about the oversight of movies. Looking back, films, especially television programs, were considered family oriented. Husbands and wives were not allowed to sleep in the same bed. If a movie scene was considered vulgar or indecent the scene was cut from the movie. There was no shame in showing a family going to church or talking about church in the movie. Some people complained about media censorship but the religious community prevailed. The majority of the national community was determined and in agreement about protecting the minds of young Americans.

The entertainment industry has sunk to new lows over the years. People barely blush when a commercial airs about sanitary napkins or enlarging one's genitals. In fact, what is blushing? Many children have been exposed to considerable vulgarity and baseness in the home because of drug addiction and alcoholism. What used to make you blush when I was a child is considered normal today.

Television is a virtual wasteland of filth, promoting adultery, fornication, homosexuality, lesbianism and everything else imaginable. What used to cause shame and embarrassment is now considered entertainment. There doesn't seem to be any restrictions anymore on what can be broadcasted on television or posted on the Internet.

Second Timothy 3:3 says that in the latter days people will become unrestrained in their behavior and guided by their emotions (i.e., suicide). There was a time when committing suicide was unthinkable because it was forbidden by major religious denominations. However, there have been increased reports of murder/suicides since the recession. We frequently hear about husbands killing their wives or parents killing their children (or vice versa) and then killing themselves. For believers, it is on Christ the solid rock we stand; all other ground is sinking sand.

Jesus said: *Surely I say to you, this generation (the whole multitude of people living at that one time) positively will not perish or pass away before all these things take place* (Mark 13:30 AMP). I believe we are the generation Jesus was referring to because we have seen many prophecies relative to the latter days come to pass. For example, the establishment of the nation of Israel, and there are also sightings of false Christ's. There has been acceleration in knowledge with the invention of the computer; it enables the usage of nuclear weapons and allows us to go to the moon almost anytime we want. Satellites are placed in the atmosphere to speed up worldwide communications; animals are being cloned and there is talk of human cloning. Jesus said regarding the things of the end of the age: *"All these are the beginning of sorrows."*

Worldly Pleasures and Sexual Immorality

When you refuse to accept God's grace and forgiveness, He will turn you loose after awhile and allow you to continue living according to your own devices. You may ultimately wind up with a reprobate (disapproval and rejected because you could not stand the test of holiness) mind. Only in the righteousness of Christ can you be approved.

The latter days may refer to such a time when people are tired of following God's righteousness and seek their own substandard way of living. The debauchery will continue until so many leave the faith that they reach a point where they won't even pretend anymore. They will cast aside the moral absolute standard of righteousness found in the Bible and form their own standard of living, such as the children of Israel did in Exodus 32 by creating an idol god (golden calf) and worshipping it instead of the true and living God.

[2]Notably, the following countries have legalized same sex marriage: Argentina, Belgium, Canada, France, Iceland, Netherland, Norway, Portugal, South Africa, Spain, and Sweden. This depravity is an epidemic that has spread to America. [3]Currently seventeen states (California, Connecticut, Delaware, Hawaii, Illinois, Iowa, Maine, Maryland, Massachusetts, Minnesota, New Hampshire, New Jersey, New Mexico, New York, Rhode Island, Vermont, Washington, and the District of Columbia) have legalized same sex marriage. What was deviant behavior is now acceptable and laws have been changed to protect it.

Not everyone agrees with the same-sex trend. Yahoo News reported in an article on March 10, 2012, that Pope Benedict XVI condemned gay marriage in a speech to bishops from the United States. According to the article, "Benedict XVI has frequently warned against liberal family values in veiled references to homosexual marriage and adoptions by gay couples, and the Catholic Church often condemns countries that recognize gay rights." I applaud the pope for taking a stand against the propagation of this ungodly trend that is spreading around the world.

The more acceptable and prevalent deviant behavior becomes in a society, the less acceptable righteousness and the fear of God is tolerated. Therefore, it is not long before deviant becomes the norm, pushing out godliness. Hence a culture or society can become like the era in Noah's time when only eight righteous people survived the judgment of God. In Sodom and Gomorrah's case there were not even 10 righteous people in the two major cities; mind you these were huge metropolitan areas of their time period.

What used to be considered the right thing to do or the way to behave is now rejected and dishonesty, greed and deviant behaviors are upheld. It doesn't seem to matter even in the court systems if the criminal committed the crime or not; what is upheld is an attorney's cunning manipulative ability to free the guilty party and of course get paid. Countless endure "white collar" bandits as they steal their way to wealth and fame while many of the righteous suffer in poverty.

Evil people who call good evil and evil good are the cause of much of the falling away from the faith that has been prophesied. People who are not grounded in the Word of God will fall prey to the devil and his schemes. Many people have lost confidence in their leaders because of the hypocrisy and corruption found in their ranks.

The need to satisfy fleshly desires for pleasure seems to be predominant globally. Some negative behaviors or what some may call "deviant," could be perpetrated because of increased drug usage. Approximately 200 million people worldwide use illegal drugs, according to a Jan. 6, 2012, blog by Katie Moisse of ABC News. It's sad to say that figure does not include ecstasy, hallucinogenic drugs, inhalants, benzodiazepines or anabolic steroids. The immorality of using drugs is now marketed as normal behavior as there are constant efforts in the U.S. to legalize the usage of illegal drugs.

The pursuit of pleasure has seduced many into believing that "pleasure" is the purpose for living. They are influenced largely by the entertainment industry whose primary goal is to push the agenda of its sponsors. The slogan in the 60s and 70s was "if it feels good, do it," so people pursued drugs, premarital sex, quick divorces, wife swapping, abortions, witchcraft and every other ungodly indulgence.

The truth of God's Word has been pushed aside by the pursuit of pleasure and replaced with the false doctrine that there are no absolute truths. This is a doctrine of devils because the Bible is the absolute Word of God to His most treasured creation—human beings. It contains all that humans need to live righteous and holy lives as planned by our Sovereign Creator.

The Seventh Commandment says: *Do not commit adultery* (Exodus 20:14 NLT). What is adultery? It is violation of the marriage covenant and vow of faithfulness that couples make to each other. Any sexual intercourse outside the marriage covenant is adultery. Jesus went so far as to say that you commit adultery when you lust in your heart, even if you don't commit the physical act (Matthew 5:27-28). Immoral thoughts can slip into your mind sometimes, especially with the amount of sexually explicit acts on television and the Internet. But deliberately viewing pornography is a violation of the marriage covenant because it is adultery if you are married and fornication if you are not.

Why is adultery wrong? Because God said so! It is wrong because it hurts people. The conscience feels a deep sense of guilt over the violation of this commandment, far beyond all the other commandments because of the covenant bond between husband and wife. Adultery cannot be justified under any circumstances.

King David understood the consequences of the sin of adultery. Not only did he commit adultery but he also murdered a man in an attempt to hide his sin. *For I recognize my shameful deeds, they haunt me day and night* (Psalm 51:3 NLT). The main reason adultery is wrong is that it destroys and undermines marriage. God values marriage so much that He established the Seventh Commandment to protect the sanctity of the first institution He created.

David's adulterous affair is found in II Samuel 11 and 12. He had Uriah, Bathsheba's husband killed in an attempt to cover up what they had done. Then he married Bathsheba probably hoping their sin would not be uncovered. You know how it was years ago when a girl got pregnant the guy would marry her so people wouldn't know about the pre-marital sexual experience. It was called a "shot gun" wedding; picture the girl's father as the one literally holding the shotgun. In David's case the baby died. God was not pleased with David and he was severely punished. David's family became very dysfunctional: his son Amnon raped his half-sister Tamar. Absalom, David's son by another wife killed Amnon to get revenge for raping his sister Tamar. Absalom later betrayed David by stealing the affections of his people and trying to take his kingdom from him. David suffered much hurt and confusion in his family as a result of his immorality.

Adultery, fornication and sex outside of marriage always hurt someone. It also hurts God because it shows a person's preference of satisfying his or her own selfish desires instead of obeying God's Word.

Immorality hurts others because it violates the commitment so necessary for a healthy relationship. It can open you up to a sexually transmitted disease and adversely affect your personality because of the lying and manipulation that takes place to hide your sin. Sexual immorality has tremendous power to destroy families, churches and communities because it destroys the integrity on which these relationships are built. God wants to protect His people from hurting themselves and others; thus, He commands that we have no part in sexual immorality, even if it is socially or culturally acceptable. Sexual immorality is a serious sin and an affront to God.

Seducing spirits attract people to their philosophies because there is little responsibility for their actions and they can continue in depravity without the thought of being judged for their acts. Hence many leave their spiritual foundational training because the lustful spirits of this world seduce them. Many of these spirits are sensual.

There is a saying in the business world that "sex sells." As such, on the cooking TV shows, some female chefs are dressed to seduce people into watching their program. Much of the advertisements have near-nude women selling their goods. All too many of the programs promote premarital sex, adultery, drinking alcohol and illicit drugs.

Be Ready Because Jesus Is Coming!

The consequences of sexual activity outside the marriage covenant are sometimes the transmission of sexual diseases (STD), infections that can be transferred from one person to another through sexual contact. According to the Centers for Disease Control and Prevention, there are more than 15 million cases of sexually transmitted disease cases reported annually in the United States. Other than HIV, the most common STDs are gonorrhea, syphilis, genital herpes, human papillomavirus (HPV), and hepatitis B. Approximately 19 million people are newly infected each year, almost half of them between the ages 15 to 24.

The human immunodeficiency virus (HIV) is the virus that infects and destroys the body's immune cells and causes a disease called AIDS, or Acquired Immunodeficiency Syndrome. AIDS occurs in the most advanced stage of HIV infection, when a person's T-cell count goes below 200 and he or she becomes ill with one of the health problems common in people with

AIDS. HIV/AIDS infection is life long—there is no cure, but there are many medicines to fight both the HIV infection and the infections and cancers that come with it. I repeat; there is no cure for AIDS.

It's sad to say but African Americans account for a disproportionate number of HIV cases. Many people don't realize they have HIV because often the symptoms don't show up for the first few years. HIV testing is the only sure way to know if you are infected. Women account for one of every four new HIV cases in the U.S. Of these newly infected women, about two out of three are African American. Most of these women contracted HIV from having sex with men who are infected. It's also reported that AIDS is now the leading cause of death for African American women ages 25-34. African American women are more than 21 times as likely to die from HIV/AIDS as non-Hispanic white women, the report says.

Contrary to what you see on television, there are no free rides—God has the best plan for the future. When you jump into bed having sex with every Tom, Dick and Harry, you will pay the consequences for violating God's commandments. Our culture encourages dating at a young age, having premarital sex with multiple partners, homosexuality, lesbianism and adultery and fornication. No one is taking responsibility for the millions of children worldwide who are born with no father in the home; nor is anyone taking responsibility for the broken hearts that are caused because of the breakup. It should be noted that the illegitimacy rate in America and Europe is approximately 50 percent. Our prisons are filled to capacity with people who had no relationship with their father. Many suffered rejection and have low self-esteem because they had no male role model in their lives. They may have felt abandoned because there was no interaction with a father figure

The story of Lot, his family, and the destruction of Sodom and Gomorrah are told in Genesis 19. These two infamous cities were located on the south portion of the Dead Sea. What were the inhabitants doing that it demanded God's judgment?

[4] The words Sodomite and Sodomy [SAHD-um-ite, SAHD uh me] are defined as: "one who practices sodomy, unnatural sexual intercourse, especially that between two males." These English words are derived from Sodom, an ancient city in the land of Canaan, noted for such depraved activities.

Lot was sitting at the gate of Sodom when two angels arrived. He recognized they were heavenly beings and bowed to the ground before them. It seems that Lot may have held a high position in the city because the city gate was a meeting place for city officials to conduct business transactions and to catch up on the latest news and gossip. Lot invited the angels to spend the night in his house but they said they would remain on the streets all night. He convinced them to return to his home for dinner. Later that night all the men of the city circled the house and called for Lot to introduce them to the two men (the angels) visiting him so they could become "familiar" with them. Lot tried to bargain with the men by offering his two virgin daughters to them. Apparently, Lot knew the perverted men would not touch his daughters because they preferred men and wanted fresh flesh, the visitors. The angels pulled Lot back into the house, blinded the Sodomites at the door and slammed the door shut. The men wanted to have sexual intercourse with the two visitors. They were unbelievably bold and daring in their actions.

Prior to Lot's angelic visitation, three angels visited his uncle Abraham and revealed to him God's plan to destroy Sodom and Gomorrah. Abraham interceded for these cities and God agreed to spare Sodom and Gomorrah if He found 10 righteous inhabitants in the cities. Needless to say, Sodom and Gomorrah were judged to be so wicked because there weren't 10 righteous inhabitants in either city. What a sad reality!

Jesus likened His return to the days of Lot: *So also [it was the same] as it was in the days of Lot. [People] ate, they drank, they bought, they sold, they planted, they built; But on the [very] day that Lot went out of Sodom, it rained fire and brimstone from heaven and destroyed [them] all* (Luke 17:28-29 AMP).

I read an article recently entitled, "Archbishop of Wales says gay marriage deserves welcome of church." Isn't that sad? Another article published in an Israeli newspaper read, "Israeli Conservative Movement Approves Ordination of Gay Rabbis."2 "In admitting gays the Israeli Conservative Movement is joining the American branch of the movement whose rabbinical seminaries have been admitting gay students for some years."

Please be reminded that: For w*e are not wrestling with flesh and blood [contending only with*

physical opponents], but against the despotisms,
against the powers, against [the master spirits who are]
the world rulers of this present darkness, against the
spirit forces of wickedness in the heavenly
(supernatural) sphere (Ephesians 6:12 AMP)

Lasciviousness

We don't hear the words lascivious or
lasciviousness often but when the Lord accuses you of
it—you are in serious trouble. Once I provided a
transition home for women that were released from
prisons and drug treatment centers. The Holy Spirit
told me to put out a particular woman immediately
because she was lascivious. At the time I didn't have a
clear understanding what the word meant. But when I
turned my radio on that morning before leaving home,
a woman was ministering on it. It means there is
nothing this person *won't* do. Of course I obeyed the
Holy Spirit and relocated her that very same day. I
discovered later that she was amoral and would not
repent or receive God's forgiveness.

[5] Look at the fleshly works of lasciviousness: It
denotes excess, absence of restraints, indecency,

wantonness, and a sin of the unregenerate that are past feelings. Lasciviousness is indecency, shameful immorality. The word is mentioned in many scriptures including, Mark 7:22; II Corinthians 12:21; Galatians 5:19; Ephesians 4:19; I Peter 4:3; and Jude 4 (KJV).

The Bible tells us: *As the One Who called you is holy, you yourselves also be holy in all your conduct and manner of living. For it is written, you shall be holy, for I am holy* (I Peter 1:15-16 AMP). Jesus gave His blood to reconcile mankind back to God. He said: *...Except a man be born of water and of the Spirit, he cannot enter into the kingdom of God* (John 3:5).

When I was growing up in the 1950s, the average American family went to church on Sundays and spent the day with their family. The stores were closed and most secular activity was shut down. However, the more affluent we became as a nation the more demand there was to open the stores on Sundays for the convenience of the people. With both mom and dad working there was more money to spend and less free time available. With the popularity of movie theaters and later television, people devoted more of their time being entertained by these visual media.

The censorship of the media that existed in the early days soon gave way to the demands of the pleasure seekers for little to no censorship. Now ball games flood the Sunday television schedules. There are those who won't go to church because their team is playing that Sunday. Slowly but surely pleasure has replaced the time normally dedicated to the things of God.

When I got saved, my church had not only Sunday morning services but also a second service after dinner, and then a night service. I was so infatuated with my newfound love that I attended all the services faithfully. Now people have less time than ever and have reprioritized church attendance to once on Sunday. As such, numerous churches have eliminated Sunday evening services and Sunday school.

A direct result of pleasure seeking is the overwhelming number of single parent homes. In some communities single parents head 70 percent of the homes. Single parents are attempting to do the job of what used to take two parents. Many, seeking instant gratification, fell out of love with the spouse of their youth and decided to obtain a quick, easy divorce and move on to their next love, leaving the responsibility for their children to someone else. This predicament is affecting the stability of Western nations.

God's commands are designed to protect us from ruining our lives and futures. God designed humans to have one partner of the opposite gender. He created Eve, a female partner for Adam, a perfect fit. The animals or beasts of the field did not fit Adam. Henceforth the prohibition against bestiality: *You shall not lie with a man as with woman; it is an abomination. Neither shall you lie with any beast and defile yourself with it, neither shall any woman yield herself to a beast to lie with it; it is confusion, perversion, and degradedly carnal* (Leviticus 18:22-23 AMP). Perverted sexual activities lead to diseases, deformity and premature death; all which disrupt family life and society.

Many people in our culture disregard what used to be the moral norm and have established a new amoral practice. But the amoral behaviors are still sin in God's sight. You are not employing God's standards if you consider them acceptable. *His thoughts are higher than our thoughts,"* (Isaiah 55:9). God tells us the consequences of sin: *But the fearful, unbelieving, and the abominable, and murderers, and*

whoremongers, and sorcerers, and idolaters, and all
liars shall have their part in the lake which burneth
with fire and brimstone: which is the second death
(Revelation 21:8). To clarify *abominable,* it means
"repulsive," "offensive," "detestable," "monstrous,"
"terrible," "awful," "horrible," "vile," "horrendous," and
"dreadful."

    Peter said the time is over for reveling in the
flesh (I Peter 4:1-6). The word *reveling* means "orgy
carousal," "noisy wild partying" or "merrymaking." The
word is used to designate any extreme intemperance
and lustful indulgence, usually accompanying pagan
worship. This behavior is unacceptable to God and
those who indulge in such uncontrollable behaviors
shall not inherit the Kingdom of God. Reveling, wild
partying and/or orgies are probably preceded by
drunkenness. When a person is excessively drunk they
become uninhibited and may subject themselves to
lascivious or lewd behavior. Loose sexuality can lead to
disease and death. The enemy will have you diseased,
imprisoned and/or dead before your time as his job is
to steal, kill and destroy as stated by Jesus in John
10:10.

Jesus hates fleshly, lustful behavior because He is preparing His Bride for His return. People who practice the sins of the flesh will not receive His seal. It's 11:59 and Jesus is coming to catch away His Bride. It is His will that none perish. *The Lord is not slack concerning his promise, as some men count slackness; but is longsuffering to us-ward not willing that any should perish, but that all should come to repentance* (II Peter 3:9). God's desire is to populate Heaven with His creation. He is a forgiving and loving heavenly Father with a wonderful plan for your life that He wants you to complete and enjoy. Carnal behaviors such as illegal drugs and alcohol addiction can hinder the development of God's plan in your life.

6 Let's examine drunkenness. The National Institute on Drug Abuse reported in an article on its website in 2011 that the cost of drug abuse and addiction (with the cost including productivity and health, and crime-related costs) tops $600 billion a year. That includes approximately $181 billion for illicit drugs, $193 billion for tobacco, and $235 billion for alcohol.

7 Why does the Lord not want you drunk or intoxicated? What does getting drunk do to you that

makes it intolerable to God? "Alcohol is made by the process of which yeasts decompose sugars in the absence of oxygen. It forms alcohol and carbon dioxide; or ethanol, wine, and beer. It can render a person semi-unconscious, or unconscious. People have reported having 'black-out' periods where they don't know who raped them, how they got home, etc., because of drunkenness. Listen to these statistics; there are more than 18 million drunks or alcoholics in America alone. Sixty-five percent of all murders involve the use of alcohol; 30 percent of all sex crimes and 35 percent of the rapes involve alcohol; 30 percent of suicides; 60 percent of all child abuse involves the use of alcohol. Eighty-five percent of all the children in foster homes are there thanks to drunkenness."

The Apostle Paul tells you in scripture how you should live: *Denying ungodliness and worldly lusts, we should live soberly, righteously, and godly, in this present world* (Titus 2:12). *Be sober, be vigilant; because your adversary the devil, as a roaring lion, walketh about, seeking whom he may devour* (I Peter 5:8).

Satan is always trying to disguise the truth of God's Word. Do not be fooled by the seemingly clean label of alcoholism or when the doctors say it is a disease. There are cultures where a glass of wine is considered part of the daily meal. There is nothing wrong with that because they are not drinking to get drunk. Individuals are called drunks who ruin their lives and the lives of others with excessive drinking. *Let us live and conduct ourselves honorably and becomingly as in the [open light of] day, not in reveling (carousing) and drunkenness, not in immorality, and debauchery (sensuality and licentiousness), not to quarreling and jealously* (Romans 13:13AMP).

The Bible further states: *Nor cheats (swindlers and thieves), nor greedy graspers, nor drunkards, nor foulmouthed revilers and slanderers, nor extortioners and robbers will inherit or have any share in the Kingdom of God* (I Corinthians 6:10). The fact that the Bible is so specific indicates that God wants you to be sober, temperate in your behavior. How can you hear the leading of the sweet quiet voice of the Holy Spirit if you're intoxicated?

Drunkenness destroys families, severs relationships, and can rob you of your job and future. Excessive drinking can cause you to lose your natural inhibitions against evil. Therefore you might gain a false boldness, have intense anger or forget the rules God put in place to protect you. Some people probably feel euphoria with an unusual rush that they have never experienced before when they take that first drink, hit of drugs or prescription drugs. Alcohol is the leading cause of various sicknesses, especially cirrhosis of the liver.

My family and I were involved in a fatal car accident that was caused by a drunk driver. We were hit at an intersection by a drunk driver who was going about 100 miles an hour. My brother's fiancée, a 28-year-old teacher who was on summer vacation, went to heaven early. The driver tried to leave the scene of the accident after he hit us. The driver of our car, my mother, was in a body cast for seven months. She never fully recovered from the emotional wounds of that trauma which took place in 1975. The angels of the Lord protected me and I was not physically injured in the accident.

Let Jesus quench that thirst. He said in John 7:37: *If any man thirst let him come unto me, and drink.* He wants His creation to be Spirit-controlled and not controlled by some foreign substance. Christians are to be sober, of a clear and sharp mind, making good, positive decisions.

Finally, the Apostle Paul said: *But Clothe yourself with the Lord Jesus Christ (the Messiah), and make no provision for [indulging] the flesh [put a stop to thinking about the evil cravings of your physical nature] to [gratify its] desires (lusts)* (Romans 13:14 AMP).

> *And [just] as it was in the days of Noah, so will it be in the time of the Son of Man. [People] ate, they drank, they married, they were given in marriage, right up to the day when Noah went into the ark, and the flood came and destroyed them all .So also [it was the same] as it was in the days of Lot. [People] ate, they drank, they bought, they sold, they planted, they built; But on the [very] day that Lot went out of Sodom, it rained fire and brimstone from heaven and destroyed [them] all. That is the way it will be on the day that the Son of Man is revealed* (Luke 17:26-30 AMP).

Reckless endangerment is the term I would use for the times in which we live. There seems to be more irresponsible and uncontrollable people than ever before. Too many will steal, rape and murder without any thought about their victim or how long they will be incarcerated. Unfortunately, they don't seem to value life as they should. To protect themselves people live behind security bars, security cameras and many carry guns to be safe from the criminal elements of society. Barricades including barbed wire fences and six-foot privacy fences are erected to keep intruders out.

Sometimes I think people have forgotten the Sixth Commandment that says: *You shall not commit murder* (Exodus 20:13 AMP). Remember the Ten Commandments are God's regulations to live by; they are not His suggestions. My definition of murder would include acts of terrorism, genocide and hate crimes that involve the taking of human life. The more prevalent the crimes the more desensitized people become toward them. Society will grow less concerned with what's happening to others around them because of multiplied lawlessness.

A major sign of the latter days is increased lawlessness. This fact is not isolated to America but is prevalent worldwide. Self-centeredness with the help of alcohol and drug addiction is fueling the increase of crime. Sadly countless people do not value life as a precious gift from God; hence the increase in suicide and murder. The sad part is multitudes of people don't realize the consequences of their attitude about sin. They are just living their lives, apathetic about living for God and do not understand they are headed to eternal damnation. The purpose of this book is to point them to Jesus before it is too late. Jesus didn't give His life for people to hurt each other. His desire is that you have life and that more abundantly: *Uprightness and right standing with God (moral and spiritual rectitude [decency] in every area and relation) elevate a nation, but sin is a reproach to any people* (Proverbs 14:34 AMP). (Brackets inserted by author.)

Pray for additional laborers who are willing to spread the message of Jesus' love and His plan for each individual's life. The signs of Jesus' soon return are flashing like a neon sign. It is later than we think. It's 11:59 and the Bridegroom is coming!

3

The Love of Many Shall Grow Cold

Just imagine, the graves will open and people's clothing will automatically drop off as they ascend into the clouds to meet the Lord in the air. I am so looking forward to this day. As a believer we can meet the Lord through the passage of death (to be absent from the body is to be present with the Lord) or with the Rapture of the Church.

But before the Rapture of the Body of Christ, Jesus said: *And the love of the great body of people will grow cold because of the multiplied lawlessness and iniquity (wickedness)* (Matthew 24:12 AMP). Parenthesis added by author.

The word *iniquity* means to have a "propensity for lawlessness," "wickedness" or "unrighteousness," which is carried through the bloodline. For example, your grandfather may have been an alcoholic and now, his son, your father, is addicted to alcohol and/or drugs. Hence, you and your siblings may have a propensity to become addicted. However you can break the iniquity by rejecting the life of addiction and by submitting yourself to the true and living God.

Growing cold as referred to in Matthew 24 occurs when people lose their love and compassion for the things of God, thus becoming insensitive, unemotional and unsympathetic to the plight of others. One of the ways the lack of love and concern for human life has expressed itself is in the form of genocide and massacres. Jesus predicted these things would happen more than 2,000 years ago and the manifestation of them are recorded throughout history. You cannot ignore these atrocities but should recognize them as partial fulfillment of Bible prophecy.

People have grown less compassionate and life has less value than it should have. Following is a partial list of events that have taken place over time that show the fulfillment of Jesus' prophecy that *the love of many shall wax cold* (Matthew 24:12).

[1]The Sudan Genocide. It is reported that 400,000 people have been killed, and more than two million have been displaced from their homes. According to the World Health Organization, the United Nations and other humanitarian agencies, an estimated 3.5 million people afflicted by the crisis are suffering from hunger. In 2004, the United States charged Sudan with genocide (Anti-Defamation League ADL). [2] In Sudan since 1985, approximately 2 million Christians have perished due to war and genocide in Sudan since 1985.

[3] In 1915 there was the Turkey, Armenian Genocide, which resulted in 1.2 million people being massacred. In the years 1915 through 1918, more than two million Armenians living in Turkey were massacred while others were forced to leave Turkey, which was their homeland under Ottoman-ruled Turkey. Notably, the Armenians were Christians.

I met a group of Armenians who owned a restaurant nearby and the owner told me about their history of annihilation and asked if Americans studied the history of what happened in Armenia. Sadly I had to admit that it was not mentioned in my history books or classes.

Adolf Hitler recognized what happened to the Armenians who were a thriving civilization for more than 3,000 years and were systemically annihilated. "After achieving total power in Germany, Hitler decided to conquer Poland in 1939 and told his generals: 'Thus for the time being I have sent to the East only my 'Death's Head Units' with the orders to kill without pity or mercy all men, women, and children of Polish race or language. Only in such a way will we win the vital space that we need."

The heart is so wicked. Jesus said: *But those things which proceed out of the mouth come forth from the heart; and they defile the man. For out of the heart proceed evil thoughts, murders, adulteries, fornications, thefts, false witness, blasphemies: These are the things which defile a man: but to eat with unwashen hands defileth not a man* (Matthew 15:18-20).

The murder and genocide of millions of people manifested itself out of evil hearts. [4]In December 1937 the Imperial Japanese Army invaded China's capital city of Nanking and murdered approximately 300,000 civilians and soldiers over a period of six weeks. [5]In

Rwanda in 1994, it is estimated that between 500,000 and one million people, or approximately 20 percent of the population in Rwanda was massacred.

The enemy of our soul is shrewd in how he creates hatred between ethnic groups over something so minor that it ignites a civil war, killing millions of people. He has no new tricks. He uses the same tactics throughout the world including America.

[6]Joseph Stalin forced the starvation of seven million people in 1932-1933. The Ukrainians call it the *Holodomor,* which means, the Hunger. "Millions starved as Soviet troops and secret policemen raided their villages, stole the harvest and all the food in villagers' homes. They dropped dead in the streets, lay dying and rotting in their houses, and some women became so desperate for food that they ate their own children. If they managed to fend off starvation, they were deported and shot in the hundreds of thousands," according to the article, "Genocide in the 20th Century." (See Stalin's Forced Famine 1932-33 7,000,000 Deaths.

[7]Last but not least, there was the Jewish Holocaust. Adolf Hitler and his regime tried to totally

exterminate the Jewish population of Europe. It is estimated that between 1941 and 1945, five to six million Jews were systematically put to death by the Nazi regime and its allies. The Jewish people have a long history of anti-Semitisms ranging from the time of their enslavement in Egypt to the present. For example under the authority of Nicholas II in 1905, thousands of homes were destroyed and hundreds of men, women and children were massacred.

Massacres and genocide of people groups are occurring today but the principal press chooses not to broadcast or publish it. Just imagine how awful things will be on earth when the Antichrist takes control. The Bible predicts in Revelation 9:18 that during the Tribulation period a third of the population will be killed. Besides that, it is predicted that the people left will be so stubborn and turned-off from God emotionally that they will refuse to repent of their murders, witchcraft, fornication and thievery (Revelation 9:21). I don't know about you but I don't want to be here during the Tribulation period.

In the latter days in which we live, man's insensitivity and inhumanity to man will continue to escalate in frequency and major events will grow in intensity the closer we approach the appearance of our Lord and Savior.

Genocide in the Womb

Webster's dictionary defines the word *abortion* as the "termination of a pregnancy after, accompanied by, resulting in, or closely followed by the death of the embryo or fetus: as a spontaneous expulsion of a human fetus during the first 12 weeks of gestation."

Millions of innocent babies have been slaughtered in the wombs of mothers. In some instances their fathers have acted as accomplices as they've sacrificed the fetuses to the gods of pleasure. Some people decide to abort their baby because the pregnancy is an inconvenience. A couple may want only one child because having more children would hinder their lifestyle. Just imagine, nations of people exterminated before they have a chance to develop into the people God planned.

Life begins at conception. God told the prophet Jeremiah: *Before I formed thee in the belly I knew thee; and before thou camest forth out of the womb I sanctified thee, and I ordained thee a prophet unto the nations* (Jeremiah 1:5).

God has great plans for every seed that is conceived and that plan is for them to be born and live productive lives. Still others have been prevented from conception by the use of birth control pills, creams and intrauterine devices.

It's 11:59 and the Bridegroom is coming!

4

Additional Biblical Prophecies

Signs in the Heavens

God created the heavenly lights—the sun, moon and stars for the purpose of giving light upon the earth (Genesis 1:14-18). He also used the stars in the heavens to direct the wise men to the location of the Christ child (Matthew 2:1-10). In addition, God uses the heavenly bodies as signs to point to His soon return. Jesus said to His disciples: *Immediately after the tribulation of those days shall the sun be darkened, and the moon shall not give her light, and the stars shall fall from heaven, and the powers of the heavens shall be shaken* (Matthew 24:29).

It is recorded in the annals of history that the sun was supernaturally darkened on May 19, 1780. Newspapers reported the following: "The 19th of May, 1780, was unprecedented in New England for its great darkness...The darkness extended over several thousand square miles."—Joseph Dorr, of Salem, Mass., History of the Town of Hampton, New Hampshire, Vol. I, p. 217. (Boston Public Library.)

Many thought that it was the fulfillment of Scripture but here we are 233 years later and the sun and moon are still shining.

The Falling of the Stars

History recorded that on Nov. 13, 1833, the stars fell from heaven. The following are several eyewitness accounts of this historical event:

> Professor Denison Olmsted, the celebrated astronomer of Yale College, said it was "the greatest display of celestial fireworks that has ever been since the creation of the world, or at least within the annals covered by the pages of history.

> "I witnessed the gorgeous spectacle, and was awe-struck. The air seemed filled with

bright descending messengers from the sky. It was about daybreak when I saw this sublime scene. It was not without the suggestion, at that moment, that it might be the harbinger of the coming of the Son of man; and, in my state of mind, I was prepared to hail Him as my friend and deliverer. I had read that the stars 'shall fall from heaven,' and they were now falling. I was suffering much in my mind,...I was beginning to look away to heaven for the rest denied me on earth." Frederick A. Douglass, *My Bondage and My Freedom,* p. 186. New York City, 1855.

Another documented observer said: "We pronounce the raining fire which we saw on Wednesday morning last an awful type, a sure forerunner, a merciful sign, of that great and dreadful day which the inhabitants of the earth will witness when the sixth seal shall be opened...A more correct picture of a fig tree casting its leaves when blown by a mighty wind, it is not possible to behold." *"The Old Countryman,"* New York. Quoted in the New York *Star* and in the Portland *Evening Advertiser,* November 26, 1833. (Portland Public Library.)

The people of the 18th and 19th centuries believed God's Word as recorded in the Bible. Thus when they saw the manifestations of the prophecies in their lifetimes they automatically knew they were living in the last days. They expected Jesus to come at any hour. These signs represented hope to believers that Jesus would make His appearance in the air and call them to their everlasting reward.

Natural disasters have occurred in every century since the beginning of time. Now people across the globe are terrorized by hurricanes, tornadoes and cyclones. These storms come from the skies. Nations all over the earth have established whether surveillances to track the monster storms and lessen any structural or human devastation.

The prophecy regarding signs in the heavens may also refer to the various satellites (communication, spy, navigation, etc.) in the atmosphere circling our planet 24 hours a day. In the 20th Century we were so intelligent that we traveled to the moon whenever we desired. It is not unrealistic to conclude this as the fulfillment of Bible prophecy.

Now when these things begin to come to occur, look up and lift up your heads, because your redemption (deliverance) is drawing near (Luke 21:28 AMP).

The Forbidding of Marriage
(I Timothy 4:3-4)

In the latter days false teachers will forbid marriage, teaching their followers that to be holy they should not marry. Others will teach abstinence from certain foods to reach a higher level of spiritual awareness. Apostle Paul wrote: *Forbidding to marry and commanding to abstain from meats, which God hath created to be received with thanksgiving of them which believe and know the truth. For every creature of God is good, and nothing to be refused, if it be received with thanksgiving: For it is sanctified by the word of God and prayer* (I Timothy 4:3-5). Paul called these teachings doctrines of devils.

Some religious organizations forbid their priests and nuns to marry. However the Bible tells us: *...It is not good that the man should be alone; I will make him a help meet for him. Therefore shall a man leave his father and his mother, and shall cleave unto his wife: and they shall be one flesh* (Genesis 2:18, 24).

If God said it is not good for man to be alone who are these false teachers to tell a young man or woman they should not marry if he or she plans on entering the priesthood? God is the highest sovereign, spiritual authority in this universe and not man made organizations.

There are those whom God has bestowed a special grace upon to remain celibate. The Apostle Paul and Jesus are two such examples. Celibacy instead of marriage should not be forced upon people. The spiritual and natural consequences resultant from forced celibacy can cause indescribable pain for individuals attempting to suppress natural inclinations.

However, single saints (male and female) must live celibate lifestyles until they marry. Their focus should be on God and His way of doing things; not on fornication, pornography, sensual appetites or self-gratification. Paul said to get married if you cannot avoid fornication (I Corinthians 7:2). Singles, it is better to marry than to burn if you cannot restrain your passions.

Forbidden to Eat Meat

Some religious sects teach their people to be vegetarians and condemn them if they are not. If they can eat meat they are forbidden to eat certain kinds of meats such as pork and various seafood. Members that participate in these formalities are made to feel they are more righteous because they abide by the Jewish Law found in Leviticus 11. But under the New Covenant Christians don't have to abide by Leviticus 11 because the Bible says there is nothing unclean of itself. According to Romans 14:20: For m*eat destroy not the work of God. All things indeed are pure; but it is evil for that man who eateth with offence.* If however eating meat offends you then you should exercise your right not to eat it. The Bible speaks for itself!

Lovers of Themselves
(II Timothy 3:2)

Apostle Paul presents a clear picture of the attitudes of the people living in the last days in his writings to Timothy. It is a vivid picture of present-day Western civilization: *For people will be lovers of self and [utterly] self-centered, lovers of money and aroused by an inordinate [greedy] desire for wealth, proud, and arrogant, and contemptuous boasters. They will be abusive (blasphemous, scoffing), disobedient to parents, ungrateful, unholy and profane* (II Timothy 3:2 AMP).

Prideful, Arrogant and Contemptuous Boasters

During my working years in the office I always tried to dress nice. I prided myself in being a pretty good dresser, while always wearing clothing according to the dress code. One day while talking to my girlfriend as we were going down the escalator, I looked at my feet. To my utter amazement I was wearing one navy shoe and one black shoe of the same style. It was an absolute embarrassment to me. Fortunately I was wearing slacks and when I stood, my feet were covered. God has a way of humbling you. Pride ends in humiliation, while humility brings honor.

That's just one example of what pride looks like. It also looks like self-righteousness, haughtiness, arrogance, ego, self-will and self-importance. Pride is a form of idolatry (self-worship); it can even take the form of competition, vanity, perfectionism and criticism. Intolerance is another form of pride, as is prejudice, self-deception, self-seduction and self-delusion.

The world system promotes all these forms of pride. But know this, God hates pride. Pride originated with Lucifer. The story of his pride is found in Isaiah 14. Lucifer was so influential that he convinced a third part of the angels to rebel against God.

Why does God hate pride? He hates it because He created humanity and wants a relationship with His creation. He wants to provide and bless you; He wants to lead you into a closer relationship with Him. Pride moves humanity away from God to self-sufficiency.

All who fear the Lord will hate evil. That is why I hate pride (the Lord says), arrogance, corruption, and perverted speech (Proverbs 8:13 NLT). Parenthesis added by author.

Proud and wicked people viciously oppress the poor. Let them be caught in the evil they plan for others. 4These wicked people are too proud to seek God. They seem to think that God is dead. (Psalms 10:2, 4 NTL).

The proud seem to think that God is nonexistent or dead. They have replaced God with their arrogance and have become gods unto themselves. They have no need to submit to a Supreme Being because the god of "self" sits on the throne.

God also hates presumption. There are times people think they are operating in faith when in fact they are operating in presumption. They want you to agree with them in prayer for a thing when they haven't been in prayer to hear the voice of the Holy Spirit themselves. They want something so they presume He will give it to them because He loves them. They presume they can manipulate God into doing what they want. God forbid. God is not a man who can be manipulated through the forces of witchcraft— manipulation and controlling people through misuse of the Word of God is witchcraft.

The children of Israel were told the consequence of disobeying God's Law: *I will break down your arrogant spirit by making the skies above as unyielding as iron and the earth beneath as hard as bronze. All your work will be for nothing, for your land will yield no crops, and your trees will bear no fruit. If even then you remain hostile toward me and refuse to obey, I will inflict you with seven more disasters for your sins* (Leviticus 26:19-21 NLT). Did you hear that? God said He will break their arrogant spirit? That tells you how much He hates arrogance.

Our God desires that we have a meek and humble spirit. Meekness—humility, quietness, modesty, mild mannered, timidity and gentleness—is a fruit of the Spirit and against such there is no law (Galatians 5:23).

Lovers of Money and Greedy for Wealth

In the last days people will be driven by greed and the hunger for more and more money will push them to do desperate things to obtain it. Greed will drive the economy and cause immorality to increase. *For the love of money is a root of all evil; it is through this craving that some have been led astray and have wandered from the faith and pierced themselves through with many acute [mental] pangs* (I Timothy 6:10 AMP).

Abusive (blasphemous, scoffing)

We are living in perilous times. The last days will be filled with people mocking each other and saying all kinds of hurtful things to deliberately cause emotional damage to someone else. Their behavior will be so abusive that the victim could be emotionally damaged permanently. For example, mean-spirited people have posted hurtful pictures and made slanderous remarks about others on the Internet that have caused people to commit suicide. Scoffing, making fun of people, and mocking is disrespectful and ungodly.

Because of the lack of religious training and respect for the things of God, people are committing sacrilegious acts against synagogues and churches. These places of worship are first being desecrated and then being burned to the ground. Priests and ministers are also being attacked and even murdered. Such blasphemous deeds are occurring in Western democratic and Muslim nations.

Disobedient to Parents (II Timothy 3:2)

The Fifth Commandment says to: *Regard (treat with honor, due obedience, and courtesy) your father and mother, that your days may be long in the land the Lord your God gives you* (Exodus 20:12 AMP). The Apostle Paul says it this way: *Children, obey your parents in the Lord [as His representatives], for this is just and right. 2 Honor (esteem and value as precious) your father and your mother—this is the first commandment with a promise-3That all may be well with you and that you may live long on the earth* (Ephesians 6:1-3 AMP).

Sadly, in these last days laws have been enacted that strip parents of their authority in the home. I grew up in a time when parents were allowed to exercise love with discipline and use the rod of correction on their children. That was a time when the government believed it was the parent's responsibility to correct and discipline their children. Even so, the Bible is still the best teacher and it says to: *Train up a child in the way he should go: and when he is old, he will not depart from it. 15Foolishness is bound up in the heart of a child, but the rod of correction shall drive it far from him* (Proverbs 22:6,15).

Today's laws tell parents how they can and cannot correct and discipline their children. The consequences of these laws are numerous. Teachers can hardly control the classroom, parents are being abused and killed by their children at an unprecedented rate, juvenile facilities are filled to capacity and the government has to build more prisons to contain undisciplined and lawless children and adults.

Unthankful, and Profane (II Timothy 3:2)

The Bible speaks for itself about people in the last days that are unthankful, unholy and profane. Let's look at the synonyms for these words for clarification of what is being said. *Unthankful* refers to a person who is unappreciative and shows no gratitude. *Unholy* can be described as one that is not set apart for God's use. They are unconsecrated, without reverence for God and may be termed secular. The word *profane* describes someone who is blasphemous, irreverent, irreligious, disrespectful, wicked and sacrilegious. Displays of such attitudes are clearly evident at every level of our society, especially in the entertainment industry and news media, Congress, educational institutions, etc.

Without Natural Affection (II Timothy 3:3)

More and more couples are deciding to live together without the sanctity of the marriage covenant vows instituted by the Church. These "common law" marriages are so numerous and popular that laws are changing worldwide to accept this ungodly behavior. Laws are being passed in some states that redefine marriage. It is no longer just between a man and woman but includes same sex couples that are legally permitted to adopt children. This governmental approval is an affront to God.

Notably, one's natural inclination is to satisfy the carnal or fleshly nature with every possible indulgence. It does not matter if God calls it a sin or unrighteous. The Apostle Paul wrote to his spiritual son Timothy about things that would occur in the last days. He said: *[They will be] without natural [human] affection (callous and inhuman)* (II Timothy 3:3 AMP). Natural affection is the love, friendliness, care and warmth that a man and woman would have for each other. However, as Paul articulated in Romans 1:18-32, God will turn all who refuse to accept and acknowledge the truth of God to their vile affections. He will turn them over to their vile affections. *26For this reason God gave them over and abandoned them to vile affections and degrading passions. For their women exchanged their natural function for an unnatural and abnormal one, 27 And the men also turned from natural relations with women and were set ablaze (burning out, consumed) with lust for one another—men committing shameful acts with men and suffering in their own bodies and personalities the inevitable consequences and penalty of their wrong-doing and going astray, which was [their] fitting retribution. 28 And so, since they did not see fit to acknowledge God or approve of Him or consider Him worth the knowing, God gave them over to a base and condemned mind to do things not proper or decent but loathsome* (Romans 1:26-28 AMP).

Apostle Paul said it more than 2,000 years ago and we now see the exhibition of these vile behaviors daily: *They will be unloving and unforgiving; they will slander others and have no self-control; they will be cruel and have no interest in what is good* (II Timothy 3:3 NLT).

We certainly see and experience this type of behavior in today's society. There used to be a time when people kept their word; in fact their word was their bond, a promise and commitment to something. That is not true today. Some believers lie through their teeth. They make commitments but you don't hear from them for years. They don't even consider honoring their contract with you; they can be cruel and have no interest in what is good. Many believers including myself have lost thousands of dollars trusting other "so called Christians." Truly we are living in the last days.

Many in the last days will have no self- control. The King James Bible calls it *incontinent,* which denotes "powerless," "impotent," and in a moral sense, "unrestrained" and "without self-control." (Vines Expository Dictionary, p. 584.) The Amplified Bible calls it *"intemperate and loose in morals and conduct,"* (II Timothy 3:3). Surely we are living in the days when some people will lose their temper and murder or attack someone for no reason at all. This unrestrained temperament is spurred by the use of alcohol, drugs or the inability to purchase drugs to feed their furious addiction.

Fierce, Despisers of Those That Are Good
(II Timothy 3:3)

Paul also describes the attitudes and behaviors of those in the last days as fierce—angry, violent, brutal, aggressive and vicious. People will hate those who are living and displaying godlike tendencies and character. They (haters) will do everything in their power to disrupt the saints, making their existence miserable.

Traitors, Heady, High-minded
(II Timothy 3:4)

Additional signs of the last days described by Apostle Paul include people who will betray each other, including family and friends. The value of loyalty will be minimized. *[They will be treacherous [betrayers], rash, [and] inflated with self-conceit. [They will be] lovers of sensual pleasures and vain amusements more than and rather than lovers of God* (II Timothy 3:4 AMP).

Many Shall Run To and Fro
(Daniel 12:4)

The prophecy that many shall run "to and fro" has been fulfilled. In Daniel 12:4 the angel told the prophet: *To the time of the end many shall run to and fro.* If taken literally we see people traveling by airplanes across the globe. Many own private jets so they have the freedom to travel at any time without being restricted by the commercial airlines and its security inconveniences. Through the manufacturing of cars we travel to and fro at will. With the use of trains, airplanes, buses, subways and cars, traveling at will is limitless. Mankind has successfully landed on the moon multiple times. Attempts are now being made to reach other planets.

Preach the Gospel to All Nations

Jesus said: *And the good news (the Gospel) must first be preached to all nations* (Mark 13:10). [2]Currently, there are 195 nations in the world. I would venture to say with the advent of airplanes, satellites, radio and television all nations have received the Gospel message. However, I doubt if all people groups have heard the Gospel message. Our job as Christians is to ensure that this prophecy is fulfilled by proclaiming the Gospel throughout the world, ensuring that every people group has the opportunity to hear and respond to it.

Knowledge Shall Increase

But you, O Daniel, shut up the words and seal the Book until the time of the end. [Then] many shall run to and fro, and search anxiously [through the Book], and knowledge [of God's purposes as revealed by His prophets] shall be increased and become great (Daniel 12:4 AMP).

Knowledge has increased exponentially since the invention of the computer. Computer technology has taken us places we have never dreamed of. The change has been so drastic that millions of jobs have vanished because of the speed and efficiency of computer technology. There have been major advancements in the medical field such that epidemics that have killed millions in previous centuries have been all but eradicated. Organ transplants have prolonged human life beyond normal expectation. Who would have thought years ago that we would be exchanging organs and even cloning animals? God only knows where that will take us.

The discovery of DNA technology has revolutionized science and biology to the point that it is possible to genetically engineer a human. Space travel to the moon and other planets is almost a standard routine. The placements of satellites in orbit around the planet provide limitless communications possibilities. The Bible says all these are the beginning of sorrows (Mark 13:8).

May 14, 1948: The Rebirth of Israel

The rebirth and establishment of Israel as an independent nation was prophesied in the Old

Testament book of Isaiah. Isaiah said: *Who has heard
of such a thing? Who has seen such things? Shall a
land be born in one day? Or shall a nation be brought in
a moment? For as soon as Zion was in labor, she
brought forth her children* (Isaiah 66:8 AMP). Zion
means Jerusalem. On May 14, 1948, more than 2,483
years after these prophecies, David Ben-Gurion,
Israel's first prime minister, announced the
independence of the State of Israel. The United States
immediately recognized Israel as a nation and Russia
followed three days later. The nation was established
as a refuge for Jews who suffered persecution in
Europe. Since then Israel has turned a desert
wilderness into a prosperous democratic republic.

It is incredible that this small nation, which
covers approximately 8,000 square miles (the size of
New Jersey), is always in the news and is always in
turmoil. The population of Israel is 7,695,000, 75.4
percent are Jews, 20.4 percent Arab, and the rest of
the population are immigrants from Russia and other
nations. About 70 percent of the population lives on a
9-mile stretch of land and the United Nations wants
Israel to relinquish more land to their enemies, the
Palestinians.

...Thus says the Lord God: Behold, I will take the children of Israel from among the nations to which they have gone, and will gather them from every side and bring them into their own land. 22And I will make them one nation in the land, upon the mountains of Israel, and one King shall be King over them all; and they shall be no longer two nations, neither be divided into two kingdoms any more (Ezekiel 37:21-22 AMP).

I was blessed to visit the nation of Israel—"The Holy Land"—in 1980; it has grown tremendously since then. We continue to pray for the peace of Israel.

Lukewarm, Contemporary Church

The Laodicean church of Revelation 3:14-22 is symbolic of today's contemporary Church. As you read this passage of scripture you'll see that God is not pleased with the complacent, compromising present-day Church. Think about your church as I paraphrase the words of Jesus below: *And unto the angel of the church of the Laodiceans write; These things saith the Amen, the faithful and true witness, the beginning of creation of God:*

- You are not cold or hot in your emotions or passion toward Me. I desire you to be one or the other. But since you are lukewarm I will vomit you out of My mouth.
- You say, "I am rich and in need of nothing." But I say you are poor, blind and scoundrels. Instead of putting your trust in earthly treasures, put your trust in My spiritual treasures.
- Pride in your achievements is nothing compared to when I open your eyes to see the truth of a right relationship with Me. Those I love, I correct and discipline.
- Before it is too late turn from your complacency and indifference and your rewards will be great in Heaven.

Jesus had nothing good to say about the Laodicean church as John described it in Revelation 3. Sadly, today's Church is more like a social club than a prayer and worship epicenter. Jesus wants His Church to be hot, on fire with passion for righteousness and not intimidated or overwhelmed by the Babylonian, worldly system. *That he might present it to Himself a glorious church, not having spot, or wrinkle, or any such*

thing; but that it should be holy and without blemish.
(Ephesians 5:27).

Affluence

Affluence can lure believers away from the faith.
Wealth will often create a false sense of security. It can
promote self-will and independence apart from the
Creator. It reminds me of the "Great Depression" era
when some investors in the stock market discovered
they had lost all their money and committed suicide.
Just the thought of being poor was enough for them to
take their lives. As previously stated, similar things
happened during the recent recession when some
people committed murder/suicide, killing both their
family and themselves. The Bible says: *For the love of
money is a root of all evils; it is through this craving that
some have been led astray and have wandered from
the faith and pierced themselves through with many
acute [mental] pangs* (I Timothy 6:10 AMP).

In Genesis 19, the writer talks about a wealthy
woman who found it difficult to leave her riches. She is
identified as Lot's wife. She probably didn't want to
leave her material possessions that she had
accumulated in Sodom and Gomorrah. When the angel

told them to run and don't look back at the two cities that were going to be destroyed, Mrs. Lot probably was lusting after the prestige and material possessions she was leaving behind. As she looked back at the burning cities she received the consequence of her disobedience and was turned into a pillar of salt.

Wealth and materialism has a tendency to give rise to pride, ego, vanity, self-righteousness, haughtiness, exalted self-importance, arrogance and intolerance. No matter how wealthy or gifted you are, God wants you to come to Him for guidance and direction.

David was a man after God's own heart. Scriptures say he was wealthy and had numerous gifts and talents. But he very rarely moved in his own strength and intelligence. Many times he would ask God, "Shall I go up, shall I do this or shall I do that?" The times when he relied on his own understanding he moved in the lust of his flesh and failed God. As a result Israel had to pay the price for his disobedience.

Can a rich man or woman go to Heaven? Can a camel go through the eye of a needle? Jesus said it is easier for a camel to go through the eye of a needle;

than for a rich man to enter the Kingdom of God. I've heard more than one minister say, "It is alright to have riches but just don't let them have you." Wealth should not be hoarded or stockpiled. Nor should it become an idol. Paul tells us to *not be conformed to this world (this age), [fashioned after and adapted to its external, superficial customs], but be transformed (changed) by the [entire] renewal of your mind [by its new ideals and its new attitude], so that you may prove [for yourselves] what is the good and acceptable and perfect will of God, even the thing which is good and acceptable and perfect [in His sight for you]* (Romans 12:2 AMP).

Apostasy—A Great Falling Away

The Western world has been rocked with church scandals that have shaken its very foundations during the 20th and 21st centuries. Some withstood the scandals and stayed in their churches while others have all but lost their faith and abandoned the church of God.

Countless others have lost their faith because their confidence was in their leaders instead of in God. Consequently, when the leader faltered their members' became disillusioned. Instead of seeking the truth of God they settled for tradition and familiarity. They have become religious robots that have a form of godliness but deny the power or authority of their faith. Solomon, the wisest man to have ever lived wrote: *Trust in the Lord with all thine heart; and lean not unto thine own understanding. 6In all thy ways acknowledge him, and he shall direct thy paths. 7Be not wise in thine own eyes: fear the LORD, and depart from evil* (Proverbs 3:5-7).

In the latter days people will lose confidence in the Church because it will resemble much of the world system. The falling away will continue to occur as leaders divorce, commit sexual immorality, manipulate finances and violate other principles of the priesthood. Some pollsters say they can find no discernible difference between Christians and those who know nothing of God. What a sad indictment on the Church of the true and living God. In the latter days there will be little hunger for righteousness or a standard of holiness; more churches will receive the stamp

Ichabod, which means, "the glory has departed," (I Samuel 4:21).

As ministries fold because of apostasy the culture will quickly become secular (worldly rather than spiritual) and Christian ethics and morality will no longer apply. Jesus said: *And the love of the great body of people will grow cold because of the multiplied lawlessness and iniquity.* [13]*But, he who endures to the end and will be saved* (Matthew 24:12-13 AMP).

Wormwood

[3] Sometimes things we consider normal and natural that occur around the world could be prophetic signs that we have overlooked. Could the Chernobyl nuclear disaster be a prophetic sign? The book of Revelation 8:10-11 speaks of a fallen star called "Wormwood" that caused many to die because it poisoned the waters.

The town of Chernobyl, Ukraine, was abandoned after a 1986 nuclear accident. *Chernobyl* in Russian means "wormwood." The nuclear accident caused a full nuclear meltdown. It was the worst nuclear accident ever. There were approximately 125,000 deaths and the radiation fallout affected about 2 million people. To top it off, it rained and the fallout from the explosion went into the ground, and the rivers and streams were poisoned.

God didn't just give us one sign of His coming, He has given us numerous signs and prophecies for His Church to heed before it is too late. *For the grace of God that bringeth salvation hath appeared to all men* (Titus 2:11). He would not leave any out of the opportunity to serve Him. However, when people reject Him by the decisions they make and the choices they live by; when they choose to bow themselves before idol gods and choose not to worship the true and living God; there is no Heaven for them. Likewise those who choose to live in immorality and practice the things God has already called an abomination, make their own decisions to follow the devil and his crowd to eternal damnation.

Evil will intensify the closer we come to the end of the age. The Ten Commandments was the accepted living standard in America and provided a clear, conspicuous line between right and wrong. Things have drastically changed. The Ten Commandments are barely mentioned, even in the Church. It seems the only time they are mentioned now is when somebody wants to remove them from public view.

Unusual Trumpet Like Musical Sounds Heard Over the World

Author Jim Paris stated in his newsletter that there have been reports since 2011 from different places in Canada, Kiev, Ukraine and America of trumpet-like sounds that can be heard for miles. Some people say they are prophetic signs. (The trumpet-like sounds can be heard on jimparisnewsletter.com under the heading "Strange Trumpet Sounds.")

It is not God's will that any should perish but that all should come to repentance. Turn from the world's system and follow the plan of God for your life. His desire is that all people be saved and come to the knowledge of the truth. Remember, the closer we come to the end, the more difficult and problematic things will be as evil intensifies.

[4]*50,000 starfish line Lissadell Beach in Ireland*

On Tuesday, Nov. 13, 2012, the Belfast Telegraph reported that approximately 50,000 starfish had come ashore overnight and perished on Lissadell beach. A picture was published by Pete Thomas, GrindTV.com. Here is another strange and unusual thing happening around the globe that could be a prophetic sign that it's 11:59.

The closer we get to the end of the age the more intense and common these unusual environmental incidents will occur.

It's 11:59 and the Bridegroom is coming!

5

The Spirit of the Antichrist

The spirit of antichrist is what I call the influence of those spiritual beings that have existed from the beginning. They followed Lucifer and rebelled against God. They aligned themselves against God and His creation, deceiving Eve. These spirits are invisible and their primary goal is to usurp God's authority in the earth. They manifest themselves as works of the flesh: pride, jealousy, murder, idolatry, rebellion, unbelief, fear, persecution, eagerness for lustful pleasure, immorality, selfish ambition, participation in demonic activities, etc. (Galatians 5:19-21, not a direct quote).

Throughout the history of the world there have been evil men who some would label the Antichrist because of the atrocities they have afflicted upon people. Some said the Antichrist was Joseph Stalin because of the millions he allowed to starve to death; while others were thoroughly convinced that he was Adolf Hitler who annihilated at least six million Jews and millions of other people. Sure enough the antichrist spirits were at work in their lives but they were not the "man of sin" that is, the Antichrist prophesied about in the books of Daniel, II Thessalonians and Revelation.

How does one recognize the spirit of antichrist? When a person does not esteem or revere Jesus as the Son of God, that Jesus is God that came to earth in human form, he has an antichrist spirit. The Bible tells us that ...*God was manifest in the flesh, justified in the Spirit, seen of angels, preached unto the Gentiles, believed on in the world, received up into glory* (I Timothy 3:16). There is only one person who fits that description, the Lord Jesus, the Messiah.

The spirit of antichrist is already operating in the world. When we look at news reports of the increased disasters, lawlessness and immorality that is happening worldwide, we can see with our own eyes and hear with our own ears that an antichrist spirit has deep roots in our society and the entire world.

You can know and recognize the antichrist spirits when worldly powers vote to remove the Ten Commandments and any other religious Christian symbols from the public arena. The spirits of antichrist exist when leaders proclaim their allegiance to activity that is clearly against God's moral laws. You know it is a spirit of antichrist when laws are passed to prevent prayers in the name of Jesus; or when history books are rewritten to delete any reference to the Christian faith of the founding fathers. When God is no longer welcomed, the doors are opened wide for evil to enter. The Bible says: *Dear children, the last hour is here. You have heard that the Antichrist is coming and already many such antichrist have appeared. From this we know that the end of the world has come* (I John 2:18 NLT).

The antichrist spirit is loose in the world and is preparing to usher in the Antichrist (a man) who will confuse and deceive the world (II John 7 NLT). *Many deceivers have gone out into the world. They do not believe that Jesus Christ came to earth in a real body. Such a person is a deceiver and an antichrist.*

Furthermore the Bible tells us there is a person called Antichrist, the "man of sin" which shall be revealed: *Let no one deceive or beguile you in any way, for that day will not come except the apostasy come first [unless the predicted great falling away of those who have professed to be Christians has come], and the man of lawlessness (sin) is revealed, who is the son of doom (of perdition)* (II Thessalonians 2:3 AMP).

Perdition means "eternal damnation" or "hell"; (the final state of the wicked).

When will the Antichrist be revealed, you may ask? The Bible says: *Dear children, the last hour is here. You have heard that the Antichrist is coming, and already many such antichrist have appeared. From this we know that the end of the world has come* (I John 2:18 NLT).

From this verse we see that John thought the world was ending in his day. He may have thought that because thousands of Christians were being persecuted, Jerusalem was destroyed again and a volcano had erupted and buried Pompeii. John had good reason to believe he was living in the last days.

At the appointed time the son of doom (perdition) whom we call the Antichrist will be revealed. The Antichrist is also known by the following names:

- Beast (Daniel 7:8; Revelation 13; 17:11)
- Lawless One (II Thessalonians 2:9)
- Man of Sin and Son of Perdition (II Thessalonians 2:3)
- Little Horn (Daniel 7:8)
- King (Daniel 8:23)

What does the Prophet Daniel say about when the Antichrist will be revealed? *At the end of their rule,* (meaning the empires mentioned in the previous verses) *when their sin is at its heights, a fierce king, a master of intrigue, will rise to power* (Daniel 8:23 NLT). Parenthesis added by the author.

God prohibited Daniel from disclosing this vision because it was for the present times. God has revealed the interpretation of Daniel's prophesies to wise men

and prophets of our time. Read all of Daniel 8:13-25; II
Thessalonians 2:8; and Revelation 19:19, 20 for
additional insight. I believe the Antichrist is alive now
and about to be revealed. However, I do not believe he
will be fully operative until after the Rapture of the
Church because the Church on earth is not mentioned
specifically after Revelation 3, when all the horrific
horrors of the Tribulation period are unleashed upon
the earth.

Only God knows the exact time when the
Antichrist will make his appearance on the world
stage. To repeat, the spirit of the antichrist is already
operating in the world because the devil and his
servants are the gods of this present world system.
Currently, there are insurrections and revolutions
happening in many nations, especially in Muslim
nations. Evil will accelerate globally the closer we
approach the appearance of the Antichrist and the
establishment of the New World Order.

The Antichrist

The Antichrist will come from among the people. For example: there are some world leaders, religious leaders and even entertainers who appeared on the world scene suddenly. One day they were unknown, and then it seemed without introduction they were known and recognized worldwide. That is how it will be with the man of sin, the Antichrist. He will make his appearance as a world leader known suddenly.

What Will Be the Work of the Antichrist?

The Antichrist will be empowered by satan. The Word of God speaks for itself and it says: ...*A king of fierce countenance and understanding dark trickery and craftiness shall stand up. 24And his power shall be mighty, but not by his own power; and he shall corrupt and destroy astonishingly and shall prosper and do his own pleasure, and he shall corrupt and destroy the mighty men and the holy people (the people of the saints). 25 And through his policy he shall cause trickery to prosper in his hand; he shall magnify himself in his heart and mind, and in their security he will corrupt and destroy many. He shall also stand up against the Prince of princes, but he shall be broken and that by no [human] hand* (Daniel 8:23b-25 AMP).

The Antichrist Will Fight
Against the Saints

*And the beast (*Antichrist author's emphasis*) was allowed to wage war against God's holy people and to overcome them. And he was given authority to rule over every tribe and people and language and nation. ⁸ And all the people who belong to this world worshipped the beast. They are the ones whose names were not written in the Book of Life, which belongs to the Lamb* who was killed before the world was made (Revelation 13:7-8 NLT).

The Antichrist Will Require People
to Receive His Mark

And he required everyone great and small, rich and poor, slave and free, to be given a mark on the right hand or on their foreheads: ¹⁷ And no one could buy or sell anything without that mark, which was either the

name of the beast or the number representing his name
(Revelation 13:16-17 NLT).

It is through this mark that the Antichrist will
be able to control the world's economy. Assigning a
number to every human being would not be difficult to
accomplish. For example, every person who is born in
the United States is automatically assigned a social
security number. The social security number is
already a national I.D. Legally you can't work in
America without that number or a work visa. Surely
other countries have similar tracking methods. There
are already methods in place and are operating to put
a chip I.D. in children, with the permission of their
parents. (See FDA approves computer chip for
humans. AP article 10/13/2004.) The ID chip could be
used to control great populations.

American believers have replaced trusting in
God with worldly methodologies. To illustrate, instead
of trusting God for our healing, the world's system
says you must take prescription medicine, be on
hemodialysis three times a week or die; or that you
must take chemotherapy and radiation treatments for
cancer. The law dictates to you that you must have

medical and auto insurance. It is mandatory even if you can't afford it.

Realistically, the Antichrist could enter the world stage at any time—if he has not already done so. The enemy will deceive many into believing that he is a regular person but there is nothing regular about him. He is a man of sin. Oh, he will say all the right things so as to be politically correct. However, in reality he is a deceiver and will persuade the world to accept his philosophies. He is lascivious (without restraint). He will be cunning, an intellectual that will amaze the world. But there is no truth in him. He will use supernatural powers given to him by his father the devil. He will even stop Christian persecution for a short time; this is just one of his ways to convince Christians that he is on their side. For a brief moment there will be a false sense of peace. Do not be deceived people of the Most High. They will cry "peace, peace" and then sudden destruction will come.

The commercial world will realign its focus and the decisions that are made will please world leaders. The "man of sin" will change and rearrange the economic climate of the leading nations to facilitate an unprecedented prosperity. There will be jobs available for all those who desire to work and there will be peace for a short time. But this peace and tranquility is only a façade. He will break trade agreements and his true motives will be exposed. However, it will be too late because the whole world will be captivated by his charismatic personality. He will even convince Christians that they don't need their Bibles anymore. Bibles will be confiscated and many will voluntarily give up their Bibles.

There will be a great falling away from the Church as it compromises the foundational standards to comply with the agenda of the Antichrist. Church members will lose confidence in the Church.

Many of the freedoms that we enjoy will be taken away from us and the American Constitution will be invalidated and replaced by the New World Constitution of the Antichrist. Fortunately, the Lord has limited his reign to 42 months—3 ½ years (Revelation 13:5).

Men's hearts are failing today because of what is happening upon the earth. Men in India are committing suicide because the market prices of grain are insufficient to care for their families. American service men returning from war are committing suicide at an unprecedented rate. Murder and suicides are happening because of the loss of employment and people's inability to pay outstanding debts; they have no hope for the future. Such bleak conditions magnified globally, is exactly the environment that would invite the presence of a dictator. Who can we get to stabilize the economic climate of the world, world leaders will ask?

The charismatic personality of the Antichrist will deceive many because he will be empowered supernaturally by satan. Through manipulation and deceit he will gain control of the world's economic systems, governmental bodies, promote a counterfeit religion, etc., for a limited time period. Nevertheless, remember that God is still in control regardless of the kind of destruction, wars, disasters or lawlessness that may come upon the earth. The Antichrist will fail as many antichrist leaders of the past. The final fate of the Antichrist and the false prophet can be found in Revelation 20:10: *And the devil that deceived them was cast into the lake of fire and brimstone, where the beast and the false prophet are, and shall be tormented day and night for ever and ever.*

Fear not, because the saints are looking for that blessed hope and the glorious appearing of the great God and Savior Jesus Christ.

Awaiting and looking for the [fulfillment, the realization of our] blessed hope, even the glorious appearing of our great God and Savior Christ Jesus (the Messiah, the Anointed One) (Titus 2:13 AMP).

It's 11:59 and the Bridegroom is coming!

6

The Holy Spirit Speaks

The Holy Spirit speaks to our spirits to warn us of things that are coming upon the earth. Things are revealed so that we will know the time of Jesus' appearance is at hand, nearer than we think. Glimpses of the present and future things that will occur are identified in this chapter. It was given to me by impressions of the Holy Spirit.

Rebellion will be rampant throughout the world in the last days. As world governments change and rearrange themselves to accommodate the new norms, there will be resistance from the status quo. Ultimately the rebellion will lead to anarchy, which will lead to wars. Resentment for not having jobs that provide a living wage, increased prices because of inflation, increased unemployment despite the pretty picture painted by power brokers and the White House will cause more lawlessness. Boycotts, work stoppages, stolen pensions and retirement savings, and distrust of the stock market will lead to worldwide famine and global discontent.

People that are accustomed to having whatever they wanted will be unable to obtain the bare necessities of life. Food, fuel and material shortages will cause worldwide panic. International and national trade agreements will be broken and protectionism will be promoted. People will lose confidence in their government because they have to work more years for less since jobs have been exported to foreign nations. As the middle class disappears, two classes will endure: the rich and the underprivileged poor. The stress will affect mostly those who have never had to struggle for their livelihood, the post *baby boomers.* Those who are more accustomed to hard work and handling difficult times will be able to manage better than the more indulged population.

Many governments will be destroyed or completely overthrown because of corruption and immorality. Lawlessness will be so inescapable that *everyone will do what is right in his own eyes.* Laws will be rewritten to reflect the prevailing mood of society therefore the population will lose confidence in the legal system. The customary laws that we have lived by according to the Bible have already been removed from the universities, and you can barely mention the name of Jesus without being insulted or criticized. As foreign money is poured into our colleges and universities, their dogma is upheld as acceptable while reading the Bible is almost taboo.

The spirit of greed and rebellion will be dignified. Those who once knew God will call out to Him for relief. Even the earth itself will cry out for relief by convulsing, even losing its shape as the competition for natural resources, i.e. fuel and food intensify. Conservation efforts will fail as the demographics of the population switch and the Western nations welcome more immigrants who destabilize the salary structure. Riots will evolve into civil wars as self-love, covetousness; murder, etc., dominate the environment. Judges 21:25 states: *In those days there was no king in Israel: every man did that which was right in his own eyes.* These are the last days!

The Holy Spirit impressed upon me
the following messages

Oct. 9, 2010

The lateness of the hour is oblivious to most people. They go about their daily tasks without any thought of God. Those that do think of Him operate in ritualistic vain repetition that is meaningless to our Heavenly Father. Jesus said in Matthew 6:7-8 *But when ye pray, use not vain repetitions, as the heathen do: for they think that they shall be heard for their much speaking. 8Be not ye therefore like unto them: for your Father knoweth what things ye have need of, before ye ask him.*

Oct.17, 2010

The hour is late and My people are still not saved. Does anyone care that the populations in the Eastern countries are not yet saved? Do My people, those who are called by My Name, care about the more than four billion people in Asia that I died and gave My blood for? Why isn't there a hunger for these souls to be brought into the Kingdom of God? These are people I want in My Kingdom. My Church does not seem to be concerned that idolaters will not enter My Heaven.

Why aren't more people going to India with My message of eternal life?

October 19, 2010

Within the next few years the world will experience more intense wars.

- There will be a WWIII
- Collapse of the U.S. and Western world economies
- Anarchy, because of the lack of finances, will affect almost everyone in the world at some point.
- People will seek death but it won't come.
- Many will give up on the churches; consequently there will be a great falling away. Their trust will be in secular humanism.
- Woe, woe unto the inhabitants of the earth
- Weeping may endure for a night but joy will come in the morning
- Those with spiritual discernment will understand that I am taking care of My business.

Nov. 7, 2010

Jesus said: *Behold, I come as a thief. Blessed is he that watcheth, and keepeth his garments, lest he walk naked, and they see his shame* (Revelation 16:15).

Jesus is telling those who are called by His name to be prepared for His arrival. It will be unexpectedly similar to the actions of a thief. A thief does not announce his arrival. He comes when no one is home or when the homeowner is asleep. In any case, the homeowner is not expecting a thief to enter his house.

The Amplified version of Revelation 16:15 says, *Behold, I am going to come like a thief! Blessed (happy, to be envied) is he who stays awake (alert) and who guards his clothes, so that he may not be naked and [have the shame of being] seen exposed!*

Believers are to keep themselves morally pure and walking in obedience to God's Word at all times. Because no one knows exactly when Jesus will come; you want to be found working in the Kingdom doing His will when He arrives.

The world will be in turmoil so it would be easy to not watch the signs of His coming and adopt the secular thinking of despair and hopelessness. Some will give up because living will become so difficult. Vigilance must be in your soul, always expecting Jesus to come at any time. Your faith and confidence must be grounded in the Word of God in the darkest hour. The Word must be hidden in your heart because you may not be allowed to have Bibles in your possession. Hide the Word in your heart that you do not sin against God (see Psalm 119:11).

Many First Century Christians suffered horrific persecution before they died. Jesus said:

Rejoice, and be exceeding glad: for great is your reward in heaven: for so persecuted they the prophets which were before you (Matthew 5:12).

Nov. 11, 2010

In the latter days, the world system will return to the wickedness that existed in Sodom and Gomorrah. Evildoers will be allowed their First Amendment rights to propagate their sexual perversion by the medium of tee shirts in schools and universities, television and music. On the other hand, Christians will be denied their First Amendment rights to display symbols of Christianity. The rights of sexual deviants to display their symbols of perversion will supersede the rights of law abiding Christians.

There will be increased persecutions of Christians throughout the world. But you will not need to fear because Jesus said: *These things I have spoken unto you, that in Me ye might have peace. In the world ye shall have tribulation: but be of good cheer; I have overcome the world* (John 16:33).

Since Jesus overcame the work of the devil and you have Jesus working in you, you have the power to overcome the world and all its evil.
Things will continue to get worse for Christians but God has given us the power to stand against evil.

Nov. 17, 2010

Morality as we know it will diminish to an all-time low. There will be so much confusion and mayhem as the Christian influence over morality will cease to exist. Satan will be loosed and his influence will dominate the thinking of popular culture. However, God will never leave Himself without a witness so there will be a remnant of Christian believers, like Lot who lived among the wickedness of Sodom and Gomorrah. Take heed. Look now at the signs of His coming. His desire is that all mankind be saved and come unto the knowledge of the truth.

> For the grace of God that bringeth salvation hath appeared to all men. 12Teaching us that, denying ungodliness and worldly lusts, we should live soberly, righteously, and godly, in this present world. Looking for that blessed hope and the glorious appearing of the great God and our Savior Jesus Christ; 14Who gave himself for us, that he might redeem us from all iniquity, and purify unto himself a peculiar people, zealous of good works (Titus 2:11-14).

Christians must live in this world but not be of the world. You must not become attached to the world's system and its way of doing things. "We must wear this world as a loose garment," the old folks used to say, knowing that our Redeemer will come at anytime to deliver us. Remember It's 11:59 and Jesus is coming.

Time is short. The evil powers are lining up against My saints but they will never prevail against My Church. It will seem for a short while that they are winning but don't be deceived—the gates of hell won't prevail against My Body of Believers. The earth will be in turmoil for the remaining years. Intense battles and struggling will ensue. But I will be a shield around My people. They will be a light to the world and especially to the enemy. They will stand on their convictions just as Daniel did when he was exiled to a foreign land.

The USA will not be the world leader as it was in the past. There will be violence in the land. Greed and corruption will drive the marketplace and debt will cause rebellion to reign throughout the land. Riots between those that have and the have not's will take place. People will yearn for peace but there will be none.

Suicides will increase because of the downward economy. Prices of goods and services will continue to escalate beyond the average person's ability to pay. The dollar will be almost worthless because of inflation. Unemployment and more demands upon the government will cause a collapse. Lawlessness and rebellion will rule the nation.

People will look for a leader who is able to solve the country's woes. There will be no place to run to because all the Western nations who have forsaken God will be in the same shape. Lawlessness and rebellion will reign in every Western country. It's 11:59 and Jesus is coming!

People will be mad at God, blaming Him for the storms and problems destroying lives and property. They will continue to mock the true and living God and curse Him. They forget that they put Him out of their schools; they put Him out of their military; they put Him out of the public square and opted for a religion without power. They worship themselves and the god of mammon and both have proven to be void of power. They refuse to acknowledge that it is in Him we live move and have our being. They have rejected the true and living God and therefore He has rejected them. It is a time when everyone does what is right in his or her own eyes. Lord, have mercy!

July 13, 2011

The latter days (the days after our Jesus shed His blood to redeem mankind back to the Father), things on earth have steadily grown worst. People have almost put God out of their lives and adopted their own righteousness. Unfortunately, this prevailing attitude exists throughout the world. Greed and addictions have driven people to murder without remorse or any thought of the consequences. The world system will not get any better but chaos will only escalate until God reaches the point when He won't tolerate any more violence.

During Noah's time: *The earth also was corrupt before God, and the earth was filled with violence* (Genesis 6:11) We have not reached this level of violence yet but we appear to be headed in that direction. The media cannot report all the violence that occurs nor can they print it all. To begin with, they are unaware of all the violence that happens worldwide. They report stories they think will appeal to the public and sell papers or increase ratings. But reading the Bible is like reading the daily newspaper. It's 11:59 and the Bridegroom is coming.

The Holy Spirit has been speaking the same word to me since 2003 concerning our country: "Hard times are coming to America." The Lord would say this to me over and over. Without a doubt there has been a recession nationally and seemingly a depression in some areas; but harder times are yet to come.

August 12, 2011

Capitalism or democracy can only survive where moral principles exist. The U.S. has survived as long as it has because of the Christian belief in God as our sovereign Ruler. That is what has kept this nation as a world leader. Solomon, king of Israel wrote: *Uprightness and right standing with God (moral and spiritual rectitude in every area and relation) elevate a nation, but sin is a reproach to any people* (Proverbs 14:34 AMP).

America used to be a fairly righteous nation. Americans used to put God first. Most of the original lawmakers were worshippers of the true and living God. Our trust in God was sown into every fiber of the society, i.e. schools, monuments, the White House and

Congressional chambers. Congressmen used to go to church and support Christianity. Even our money carries the inscription "In God We Trust." Righteousness exalts a nation, especially America.

There was a time in America when people borrowed something they were obliged to pay it back. A deal would be sealed with a handshake. A person's word was his bond. There was a time in the classroom when you would open the day with prayer and close it with prayer, or in some classes, a song.

Our family didn't have a lot of money but we were happy with the love we shared. I never had a new bike or a bike of my own. My parents refurbished a bike that my three sisters and I had to share. We were happy and content with what we had.

March 13, 2012

God's Glorious Church

The urgency to write the book "It Is11:59" is because Jesus is coming sooner than people think. He does not want His people to be caught off guard. He is looking for a glorious church without spot or wrinkle— no impurities. Of course the only way that it can happen is when He catches away His Church. When the Church is lifted all impurities will be left on earth.

Human beings cannot do anything themselves to be pure enough for Heaven. Jesus has already paid the price with His blood to atone for sin. So when He said He's looking for a glorious Church He's not looking for human works, the price has already been paid.

He's looking at the heart and for those who have accepted the atonement of Jesus for their sins.

March 16, 2012

- President Obama will be re-elected.
- Hatred against African Americans will increase and become more brutal.
- There will be race riots, Latinos, blacks, whites and much turmoil in the streets of America.
- Unprecedented double digit inflation
- Instability in every area
- Government in-fighting
- Those who have will oppose those who have not

- Persecution against the church because of its stand against homosexuals
- Everybody is doing what is right in his own eyes

My Dream

It was a beautiful sunny clear day and my granddaughter and I were walking through a desert hill area. All of a sudden we turned around and what seemed like a battalion of army troops were trailing us. The soldiers not only had rifles and other weapons but they had heavy artillery guns and were chasing us. The ground was void of greenery; it was sandy and mountainous. We ran into a shallow cave to seek refuge. As we entered the cave the enemy soldiers lined up their artillery guns facing the mouth of the cave. I could see the commander of the army lifting up his arm to signal the soldiers to start shooting at us as we stood shivering and shaking in the cave. The commander lowered his baton giving the orders to commence firing at us. The cave was so shallow that they could see us in the mouth of the entryway. But as soon as the shells came through the mouth of the cave, they dropped to the ground in front of us. It was like a force field was surrounding us, preventing the giant artillery shells from hitting us. Instead the shells dropped in front of us. None of the enemy's fire could touch us. I heard the words "Holy Spirit protection." It reminded me of the words found in Isaiah 54:17: *No weapon that is formed against thee shall prosper; and every tongue that shall rise against thee in judgment thou shalt condemn. This is the heritage of the servants of the LORD, and their righteousness is of me, saith the LORD.*

God's umbrella of protection was a shield about us and the weapons of the enemy were unable to penetrate the shield that God provided around us. It was a miracle of God that caused the huge artillery shells to hit the invisible wall of protection about us and to fall before our very eyes to the ground. I never forgot that dream because it was so realistic. God is a miracle working God who is able to perform great exploits to save His elect.

In the latter days there will be civil wars in many countries as well as wars between nations. Nations will war against its neighbor as the "man of sin" attempts to conquer the world. It seems like peace will be taken out of the earth. However my dream reinforces that God will protect His elect. The time is 11:59 and the devil is angry because Jesus is coming.

World War III (Holy Spirit Message)

There will be another world war. This war will be a fight for the world resources, oil, and other natural resources, i.e. timber, fresh water, mineral deposits, gold and silver. There will be a redistribution of wealth. The first will be last and the last will be first. Countries that didn't do well after WWII will be the new leaders. China will dominate the Western nations because of the huge debt owed them. The borrower will become servants of the lenders. The only thing the West has to bargain with is its natural resources. The dollar will become less valuable because of inflation.

It's 11:59 and the Bridegroom is coming!

Miscellaneous

"Sandra, My daughter, you must tell My people that time is running out and My grace will not last forever. I will continue to uproot and reveal more hypocrites in leadership in My Body (Church) and in politics. There is corruption at every level of government, religion and within major corporations; don't be surprised what is revealed. Don't get caught up in the gossip of it all. Corruption and greed will be exposed in the political parties. Don't be surprised when it is exposed.

Hard times will come to America; anarchy, disorder and confusion. After a society reaches a level when it throws out its foundational truths that have sustained it for many years and replace them with vein philosophies and deviant behaviors, that society has set itself up for judgment. Another group of people acted similarly according to Judges 21:25: *Every man did that which was right in his own eyes.*

People, I repeat, "It's 11:59 and Jesus will come at midnight." If Christians don't separate themselves from the world's system, they will be caught up in it.

Once the slope starts to slide it is not easy to recover from the inertia.

One purpose of the Bible is to show people how history repeats itself. We must learn from past failures and not repeat the evils and injustices if possible. If people won't learn from history they will repeat it and be judged for their disobedience.

Apostasy will continue but will grow in intensity. Whole organizations will fall like massive earthquakes, similar to the 2004 tsunami in South East Asia when 227,898 people died. My representatives will fall like dominoes.

So apostasy is to be expected because the Holy Spirit has already announced it. The falling away from the faith will affect believers and non-believers.

Jeremiah 8:20 says it this way: *The harvest is past, the summer is ended, and we are not saved.* Where are the laborers?

Then saith he unto his disciples, The harvest truly is plenteous, but the labourers are few. [38] Pray ye therefore for the Lord of the harvest, that he will send forth labourers into his harvest (Matthew 9:37-38).

Jesus' coming is imminent. Therefore it behooves this generation to stop wasting time with the things of this world and do the things that He desires. His longing is to populate Heaven but He works through people. You must look beyond your borders and gain a Christ perspective for the world population. It is not about you, it is about souls. You will be held accountable if you don't develop a worldview of the things of God.

What are some things you can do to develop your mind to view things from God's perspective?

- Research those Christian organizations ministering globally and support them financially and with prayer.
- Pray fervently (hot and passionate prayers) for the lost (non-believers) and for more laborers to reach the masses.
- Ask God to show you how to reach the masses.
- Support those ministries that convert non-believers, not just feed them, in other countries.

- Seek God for a specific country He wants you to focus your attention.

The reason I shared these things with you is not to depress you but to equip you. You must be prepared because Jesus predicted that all these things would happen. I'm merely reiterating what He has already said. I don't want you to be caught off guard. The time to stand for God is NOW! Wake up Church and stop being put to sleep with false messages on television and new laws that sexual immorality (fornication, adultery, lesbianism and homosexuality) is permissible. It is allowed in satan's kingdom but it is not allowed in Heaven's. God is holy and will not tolerate any sin in His the Kingdom.

The offer of salvation through the shed blood of Jesus Christ is offered to all people regardless of nationality.

Watch ye therefore and pray always, that ye may be accounted worthy to escape all these things that shall come to pass, and to stand before the Son of man (Luke 21:36).

It's 11:59 and the Bridegroom is coming!

7

How to Face the Future

God's reason for revealing signs to you is not to terrify you but to alert you to the fact He is soon to return. The signs are everywhere, just open up your eyes and look. Jesus wants you to be prepared and ready to go when He calls for you. He redeemed you from the hand of the enemy when He shed His blood on the Cross. Your dwelling place is being prepared in Heaven and rewards are awaiting the saints as compensation for obedience to His will during your lifetime.

However, no one but the Father knows when the Church will be caught away. Jesus likened the end times to the great flood. When the flood came it was a sudden cataclysm that fell upon all the earth's inhabitants and destroyed the unbelievers. Noah tried to warn the people that God was going to destroy the earth because of their wickedness. However, to my knowledge, the only signs that materialized to help them understand that things were about to change were the boat that he was building. He preached for 120 years, warning of the coming destruction (II Peter 2:5) but there were no converts (I Peter 3:20).

Noah's exemplary life stands as an example for us that in spite of the debauchery that covered the world around him, Noah remained faithful to God. He did not allow himself or his family to succumb to the evils of his day. The story of Noah and the flood is found in Genesis 6-8.

The writer of Hebrews declares:

[Prompted] by faith Noah, being forewarned by God concerning events of which as yet there was no visible sign, took heed and diligently and reverently constructed and prepared an ark for the deliverance of his own family. By this [his faith which relied on God] he passed judgment and sentence on the world's unbelief and became an heir possessor of righteousness (that relation of

*being right into which God puts the person
who has faith)* (Hebrews 11:7 AMP).

As our world continues its downward spiral,
Christians are to be aware of what is happening
around them. Here are a few tips:

- Saints should mutually strengthen, encourage
  and comfort each other according to their faith.
- If you have wandered away from God's way of
  doing things, reestablish yourself with God;
  separate yourself from all that hinders your
  spiritual growth.
- Make a conscience decision to learn from the
  past. Then forget those things that are behind
  and reach forward to those things that lie ahead
  (Philippians 3:13).
- You are being changed from glory to glory; get
  back to focusing on being like Jesus and be
  open to what the Holy Spirit has to say.
- Occupy, stay busy, productively doing the work
  of the Lord that He has called you to do.

God loves humanity so much. It is not His will that
any should perish. He did not create eternal

damnation for mankind. It was designed for the devil, his angels and followers.

The closer it comes to the Rapture, the more lawlessness and immorality will intensify. Saints will be under tremendous pressure to renounce their alliance to Jesus. Some saints will suffer persecution. James declares: *Blessed (happy, to be envied) is the man who is patient under trial and stands up under temptation, for when he has stood the test and been approved, he will receive [the victor's] crown of life which God has promised to those who love Him* (James 1:12 AMP).

Trust the scriptures during the difficult and dangerous times and put no confidence in your own understanding. Seek God about everything, knowing that the deceiver wants to trick you into following after him. Always remember you are in a war and must be vigilant at all times because the enemy seeks to steal what is yours, kill and destroy you. He will use whatever weapons available to distract you from your godly assignment (your thoughts, social media, political allegiances, loved ones, how you spend your time, friends, entertainment, coworkers, the economy, pleasures of this world, etc.) to destroy you. Trust the Word of God to help you stay focused on Him. Always remember, God is in control! Jesus said He is the first and the last; the beginning and the end.

Regarding the Death of a Loved One

Death is certain as long as you are in this earthly body. The grief over the death of a loved one can feel like an attack by an unbearable pain for which there is no treatment; nothing manmade can quench the awful hurt on the inside of you. For those who must be in control of every circumstance, sudden death can surely strip your dominance.

Unfortunately, for non-believers the transition of a loved one may trigger anger and resentment toward God blaming Him for allowing death to touch their life. Because they don't understand the Word of God, they may experience feelings of hopelessness about the fate of the departed one. But once it is realized that God is still in control of the universe and beyond, then they can accept the hope Apostle Paul gives us. He states in (I Thessalonians 4:13-18):

1) Your loved one is not permanently gone, but sleeps. You know that sleep is a temporary state. There is reason to hope because Jesus conquered death when He died and rose again to new life and is in Heaven now.

2) Those who perished believing that Jesus died and rose again will come with Him when He comes for His Church (Rapture). In fact, they will be the first to meet Jesus in the air.

3) Now is the opportunity for the non-believer to accept the salvation that Jesus offers. Whoever believes in Him will have eternal life with Him in Heaven.

4) When the trumpet sounds the new believer will meet their loved one in the air and so shall they be with the Lord!

So saints, be comforted by the words of Paul because Heaven is your home.

8

Conclusion

Those who have had the good fortune to visit Heaven have brought back wonderful stories of their experience. But the one thing that is consistent in their stories is the message to tell those on earth: "Jesus is coming!"

John told us that same truth in the book of Revelation more than 2,000 years ago and it is still being told today. That means His return is more imminent now than ever before. All the signs point to His return. The fact that the Holy Spirit gave me the title of this book "It's 11:59 and Bridegroom is Coming" is evidence of His desire to warn people of His soon return. Apparently He wants people to know His return is at the door. He loves humanity so much. It is not His will that any should perish but that all men be saved and come into the knowledge of the truth.

Many are still waiting for the predictions of pandemics, wars and rumors of wars to be fulfilled. Hopefully after reading this book you will see as I've traced history and noted, many of these atrocities have already occurred and will continue with a greater degree of intensity and frequency as the time of His return draws near.

Heaven is warning us so that we will labor in the field reaching multitudes with the "Good News" while it is still day. Jesus is still our example. My brothers and sisters I admonish all to do the work of the Lord while there is still time.

The warnings of Jesus' soon appearance is for us to live a lifestyle that is honorable and holy as unto the Lord. He will come as a thief in the night. The world's system will continue moving along in its decadence and self-indolence just like in Noah's time just before the floodwaters consumed them. I'm sure the inhabitants had many warnings of the pending destruction that was coming but continued to live in self-denial. Jesus said: *Watch therefore: for ye know not what hour your Lord doth come. ... ye also ready:*

for in such an hour as ye think not the Son of man
cometh (Matthew 24:42, 44).

God is looking for those who are prepared as
evidenced by their obedience and faithfulness to Him.
Maintain Him as your first love and don't compromise
your faith. The pleasures of this world are not worth
losing your eternal life with the Savior Jesus.

The way to safety is through trust in the shed
blood that Jesus paid on the Cross of Calvary for the
forgiveness of humanity's sin. Trust in and obedience
to the Word of God will lead to living an eternity with
the Father in Heaven. As from the beginning of time
God's Word will continues to be fulfilled. The enemy of
your soul will continue to cause disagreements,
leading nations into wars, stirring up storms in the
seas and oceans, and initiating the spread of new
diseases. These events will continue and intensify until
the trumpet is sounded for the Church's departure.

My purpose for writing this book is to wake up
lackadaisical, lukewarm Christians and non-believers
to the truth that Jesus is at the door. Irrespective of
prophecies yet to be fulfilled, I am excited about the
future. I look forward to the future revivals as
multitudes are going to be saved because the Body of

Christ will be accelerated to spread the Gospel message to every nation, tongue and people.

"It's 11:59 and the Bridegroom is Coming" is not a message of gloom and doom, it's a dispatch of hope and expectancy of our coming Savior Who is alerting His people to their soon homecoming celebration. It is not for them to be fearful but that they will be ready and not caught off guard.

Just think, our mansions are ready and awaiting our occupation. The angels are standing guard ready to blow the trumpets to summons us to be with the Lord. Our sovereign God is still in charge and will have the ultimate victory. Therefore, I am comforted by His faithfulness and the manifestations of His promises. What He promised will surely come to pass. It's 11:59 and the Bridegroom is coming!

Salvation Plan

It is God's desire to populate Heaven with His creation. It is God's will for all mankind to be saved, and come unto the knowledge of the truth (I Timothy 2:4).

Jesus said in John 3:16: *For God so loved the world, that he gave his only begotten Son, that whosoever believeth in him should not perish, but have everlasting life.*

- Repent. Acknowledge that you are a sinner. Pray and ask God to forgive you of all unrighteousness (the sins you have knowingly committed and those you have committed unknowingly).

- Confess that Jesus is the Lord. The Bible says in Romans 10:9-10, 13: *That if thou shalt confess with thy mouth the LORD Jesus, and shalt believe in thine heart that God hath raised him from the dead, thou shalt be saved. For with the heart man believeth unto righteousness; and with the mouth confession is made unto salvation.*

- *For whosoever shall call upon the name of the Lord shall be saved.*

- Pray this prayer:

- *Jesus, You are my Lord and Savior. I come to You just as I am, a sinner. I confess I have sinned against You in thought, word and deed. Please forgive me of all my wrongdoings, and cleanse me of all my unrighteousness. I believe in my heart that God raised You from the dead. By faith in Your Word, I receive salvation now. I submit my life to You today. Help me to live my life pleasing to You. Thank You for saving me.*

- Ask God to lead you to a Bible-believing and teaching church of His choice.

- Get baptized (immersion in water) in the authority of Jesus.

- Believe that you are a born again child of God. Now walk in your renewed mind by changing your mindset from the world's way of doing things and begin to live for God and His way of doing things.

All of Heaven applauds your decision to make Jesus first in your life!

Notes

Chapter One

1. http://www.roman-empire.net/maps/empire/extent/rome-modern-day-nations.html. Assessed August 20, 2012.

2. "Countries in the EU, assessed January 3, 2012. http://www.userfocus.co.uk/eu.html.

3. Those who claim to be the Messiah and those who claimed to be Jesus. http://en.wikipedia.org/wiki/List_of_Messiah_Claimants. 4/8/2010. en.wikipedia.org/wiki/List_of_people_who_have_claimed_to_be_Jesus 4/8/2010).

4. Werstein, Irving 1914-1918: World War I. The New Book of Knowledge, p.270-281.

5. S.L.A Marshall, World War II. The New Book of Knowledge, p. 282-308.

6. Atomic Bombings of Hiroshima and Nagasaki. http:/en.wikipedia.org/wiki/atomic bombings of Hiroshima and Nagasaki assessed 4/9/2010.

7. Time Almanac 2010. P. 160-161.

8. http://www.washingtonpost.com/blogs/capital-weather-gang/post/venice-flooding-sw...viewed11/15/2012

9. Yahoo News 4-29-10.

10. http://www.edc.gov/ncidod/eid/vol 112no)1/05-0979.htm. 4/2/2010.

11. http://virus.stanford.edu/uda/The Influenza Pandemic of 1918. Viewed 08/31/2013.

12. (pajamasmedia.com/phyllischesler/2009/08/12/open-season-on-christian.)

Chapter Two

1. Peterson, Frank Lois. The Hope of the Race. Southern Publishing Association. Nashville, Tennessee. 1946. P.232

2. http://en.wikipedia.org/wiki/Same-Sex_marriage

3. http://en.wikipedia.org/wiki/Same-Sex_marriage_in_the_United_States. Viewed 4/2/2012

4. Youngblood, Ronald F. General Ed. Nelson's New Illustrated Bible Dictionary (Sodomite). P.1189.

5. Vines Expository Dictionary of New Testament Words (lascivious) p. 640.

6. http:www.drugabuse.gov/infofacts/understand.htm
   l

7. Watkins, Terry. Dial the Truth Ministries. "The
   World Deadliest Drug."
   http:/biblebelievers.com/walkins_alcohol.html.

8. "Archbishop of Wales says gay marriage deserves
   welcome of church."
   http:/www.walesonline.co.uk/news/wales-
   news/2012/04/18/archbishop-of-wales-says-
   gay...4/20/2012

Chapter Three

1. www.adl.org/Sudan. [Anti Defamation League]

2. Jesus Freaks. "Sudan." Bethany House Publishers,
   Minneapolis, MN 55438. 1999. P.349.

3. www.historyplace.com/worldhistory/genocide/arm
   enians.htm

4. http://www.historyplace.com/worldhistory/genoci
   de/nanking.htm. 4/25/2010

5. http:/en.wikipedia.org/wiki/Rwandan_Genocide.
   4/25/10.

6. www.historyplace.com/worldhistory/genocide/stlin
   .htm.)

7. www.dailymail.co.uk/news/worldnews/article-
   1038774/Holocaust-hunger.4-25-10.

8. http://www.historyplace.com/worldhistory/genoci
   de/holocaust.htm 4/3/2012

Chapter Four

1. Peterson, Frank Loris, The Hope of the Race.
   Southern Publishing Association, Nashville,
   Tennessee.1946. "Signs of His Coming" p. 219-224.

2. www.infoplease.com/ipa 4.7.2010).

3. http://www.ibiblio.org/expo/soviet.exhibit/cherno
   byl.html

4. http://www.grindtv.comm/outdoor/41673/mysteri
   ous+stranding+on+irish+beach+onvo..viewed
   11/15/2012

Appendix

Everlasting or Eternal Life Scriptures

Job 19:25-27

Matthew 16:25, 26; 18:8; 19:16; 19:29

Mark 3:29; 10:17

John 3:15-16; 6:40; 10:28; 14:3

I John 2:25; 3:15; 5:11

Romans 6:23

I Corinthians 15:51-52

I Thessalonians 4:17

I Timothy 6:12

2 Thessalonians 1:9

Jude 21

Revelation 22:5

About the Author

The Lord has blessed Sandra H. Moore with the spirit of compassion and a heart for the lost. She has traveled extensively throughout the world on short-term mission trips in Jamaica, Ghana, Zimbabwe, Moscow, Beijing and Canton, China, the Australian Outback, and in New Zealand.

Sandra is also a deliverance and inner healing minister. She believes Christians who receive inner healing and deliverance are more effective to the Body of Christ.

"Obedience is Key" is the name of her weekly radio broadcast. The broadcast airs on 1440 AM WDRJ radio station.

Sandra received a Master of Theology from Destiny Christian University and graduated from the University of Detroit Mercy with a Bachelor of Arts degree.

She is the author of *Obedience Is Key to God's Blessings* and *Reaping God's Blessings*. Sandra is the widow of Earl D. Moore, lives in Oak Park, MI and has an extended family of two daughters, a son, and grandchildren.

Sandra H. Moore can be reached at:

P.O. Box 470340
Oak Park, MI 48237

BOOK ORDER FORM

It's 11:59 and the Bridegroom is Coming!

By Sandra H. Moore

Name _____

Address _____

City _____ State _____ Zip _____

Phone _____ Fax _____

Email _____

Quantity	
Price *(each)*	$12.99
Subtotal	
S & H	$1.99
Additional copies	
TOTAL	

METHOD OF PAYMENT:

❏ Check or Money Order (***Make payable to***: **Sandra H. Moore**)
❏ Visa ❏ Master Card ❏ American Express
Acct No. _____ CVV _____
Expiration Date (*mmyy*) _____
Signature _____

Mail your payment with this form to:
Evangelist Sandra H. Moore
P.O. Box 47034
Oak Park, MI 48237